BOURNEMOUTH
THEN MEETS NOW

by Rodney Legg

HALSGROVE

First published in Great Britain in 2009

Copyright © Rodney Legg 2009

British Library Cataloguing-in-Publication Data
A CIP record for this title is available from the British Library

ISBN 978 1 84114 758 1

HALSGROVE
Halsgrove House,
Ryelands Industrial Estate,
Bagley Road, Wellington, Somerset TA21 9PZ
Tel: 01823 653777   Fax: 01823 216796
email: sales@halsgrove.com

Part of the Halsgrove group of companies
Information on all Halsgrove titles is available at: www.halsgrove.com

Printed and bound by Grafiche Flaminia, Italy

CONTENTS

Introduction 4

Alum Chine 6
Stevenson Memorial Bridge 8
West Overcliff Drive 10
Middle Chine 12
Durley Chine 14
West Cliff 16
The Beach (Westwards) 18
Pier Approach 20
Bournemouth Pier 24
The Beach (Eastwards) 28
East Cliff 30
East Cliff 32
East Cliff Zig-Zag 34
Cliff Lifts 36
Pier from the East Cliff 40
East Cliff Hall 42
Carlton Hotel 44
Boscombe Pier 46
Boscombe Pier Approach 50
Boscombe Chine 52
Honeycombe Chine 54
Fisherman's Walk Beach 56
Southbourne Pier 58
Hengistbury Head 60
Tapps Arms Inn 62
Central Station 64
Omnibus and Coach Station 66

The Square (Looking West) 68
The Square (Looking East) 72
Exeter Road 76
Winter Gardens 78
Beales 80
The Lansdowne 82
Lower Gardens 84
Children's Corner 86
Invalids' Walk 88
The Pavilion 92
Manor Road 94
St Peter's Vicarage 96
Poole Road 98
Horseshoe Common 100
Meyrick Park 102
Crescent Gardens 104
Boscombe Hill 106
Royal Arcade 108
Holy Trinity Church ...110
Bournemouth Natural Science Society 114
Charminster (and Queen's Park) 116
Holdenhurst 120
Pig Shute 124
Riddlesford 126
Tuckton Bridge 130
Wick Ferry 132
Talbot Village 136
The Moderne 140
Wimborne Road Cemetery 142

INTRODUCTION

Bournemouth's shield and motto: 'Beauty and health'

The Bournemouth we know is a Victorian new town. As a place-name, however, it can be traced back to 'la Bournemouthe' in the Christchurch Cartulary of 1407. Bournemouth, as an area, comprises four tithings (Holdenhurst, Muckleshell, Muscliff and Throop) in the chapelry of Holdenhurst, plus two tithings (Tuckton which included Wick and Iford which included Pokesdown) in the parish of Christchurch. The parish of Kinson was transferred from Dorset by the Bournemouth Corporation Act, 1932. The County Borough of Bournemouth remained part of the county of Hampshire until boundary changes under the Local Government Act, 1972, handing it to Dorset, which came into effect on 1 April 1974.

The pictures here have come from four sources. Those my father took. Those I have taken. Postcards collected by him and by me. Other photographs we were given, such as lantern slides by Bournemouth solicitor Edwin Dodshon.

The words are a mix of the factual as potted biographies of people and place and contemporary quotations from the backs of postcards. These were the text messages of their day and record the minutiae of everyday life that historians usually miss. Their other virtue is that they give us a random sample of visitors to Bournemouth as a seaside resort, what they were doing, and how life is treating them.

Offshore, to us it is Bournemouth Bay, but officially it remains Poole Bay for the shipping that enters and leaves Poole Harbour has to use the passage between Sandbanks and Shell Bay. In laying out the archive I've chosen four basic background colours, though often the shades are a mixture to reflect overlapping components.

- Blue zone – the sea
- Yellow zone – beaches and cliffs
- Green zone – parks and riverside
- Orange zone – the town

I've started with the main attraction – the sea – and then moved inland to the central shopping areas and a glimpse at the suburbs, to finish with open spaces and a cemetery.

My all-time favourite Bournemouth quotation comes from our own times, when Home Secretary Jack Straw visited a nursing home, during the Labour Party Conference in October 1999. Having asked an elderly resident if she knew who he was, Straw was told:

'No dear, but if you ask Matron she will tell you.'

Cutting from the *New York Herald* in the 1930s: **'Bournemouth has the best climate in the British Isles and a perfect beach.'**

Cutting from the *Manchester Guardian* in the 1930s: **'Bournemouth is proud of having devoted more than a tenth of its space to parks and gardens.'**

Sir Kingsley Wood, Minister of Health, on 8 October 1936: **'Bournemouth is one of our most popular health resorts, and will, of course, always continue to be, possessing as it does, an equable climate and healthy and delightful surroundings. It is a great pleasure for me to visit it again where I spent so many happy days, and where I hope to spend many more.'**

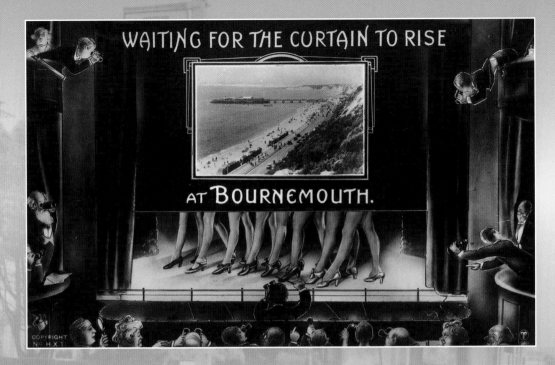

End of the pier show in the 1920s

Town centre poster, 2008, of new-look
Bournemouth courtesy Jeff Pigott and
Year-5 children at St Michael's School

ALUM CHINE

This deep-cut dry valley takes its name from a chemical used in medicine and the arts. James Blount, 6th Baron Mountjoy, lord of the manor of Canford, took over an alum-making patent for copperas and alum supply. The source was on the Isle of Wight under the famous coloured sands of Alum Bay and Mountjoy then opened similar mines on his own estate which stretched from Wimborne to the sea and shared the same Bagshot Beds geology. In the process he lost a fortune and Alum Bay and Alum Chine were left to revert to nature, amid pine plantations which dated from the turn of the nineteenth century.

Colonial administrator and poet Sir Henry Taylor enthused over Alum Chine and the nearby 'Marine Village':

> 'The place is beautiful beyond any sea-side place I have ever seen except the Riviera, and the air is dry and pure, unacquainted with anything but sea, the pine woods, which reach for miles inland, and the sandy soil in which they grow.'

He proceeded to vote with his feet and built The Roost (later named Rawden) in Hinton Road, in 1861. Taylor's fame rested on a single work, *Philip van Artevelde* in 1834, which did for drama what Sir Walter Scott had achieved in the novel. In Bournemouth, in sunny microcosm, he saw a romantic landscape that could be celebrated with the enthusiasm of a Wordsworth for the

Alex Austen's painting of Alum Chine for an Edwardian 'Rapco' postcard

From the same spot in 2008

6

After the arrival of the promenade, in 1933

Scrubbed-up, from the clifftop in 2008

Lakes. Cosmopolitan men of letters came by train to The Roost. They included Thomas Carlyle, Dean Church, Benjamin Jowett, Alfred Lord Tennyson, and Aubrey de Vere.

The rustic look at Alum Chine was doomed from 20 March 1903 when as from the previous year, landowner Sir George Meyrick signed over the cliffs and foreshore to Bournemouth Corporation in a 999-year lease. It had long been a live issue because cliff-falls were threatening the luxury lifestyles of those living above. The Undercliff Promenade headed this way from Bournemouth Pier, in 1910, with the section beside Alum Chine being built in 1912. Seaside paraphernalia followed, give or take interruptions and removals, caused by two world wars. Whether Sir Henry Taylor would still see beauty is arguable.

Punch & Judy on the beach

Bennett Beale, who grew up in Alum Chine Road and left school in 1895: **'Our playground was usually the roadway outside the house, or the common, and the chines of the West Cliff, and in the Nineties we saw with dismay the preparations for road making and after that the building of many large and expensive houses there.'**

Card to Mr A. Barker in Windsor Road, Boscombe, 8 September 1903: **'This is rather a pretty place.'**

Mary to Miss Teague in Manor Park, London E, 3 April 1906: **'The weather is glorious, sun broiling today & a perfect sky & the sea lovely.'**

Raphael Tuck & Sons' Oilette postcard caption, 1911: **'A chine is the local name for a ravine. Bournemouth has several beautiful chines, one of its largest being Alum Chine. Nearly a mile long, it is well laid out, so that the visitor need not exhaust himself in realising its charm. It takes its name from the tradition that alum was once manufactured in this district.'**

Elsie to Miss G. Gaymer in Shepherds Bush, 21 June 1918, on a card stamped 'BUY NATIONAL WAR BONDS NOW': **'We walked to this very pretty chine on Sunday morning and enjoyed the walk very much.'**

The view from Alum Chine in 1905

Still an open view in 1910

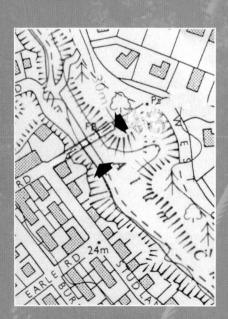

STEVENSON MEMORIAL BRIDGE

The Victorian rustic bridge across in the middle of Alum Chine was replaced in 1904 by a steel suspension bridge, named the Stevenson Memorial Bridge for Robert Louis Stevenson (1850-94), who wrote *Kidnapped* in a villa in sight of the spot. This pedestrian bridge is a direct continuation, eastwards, of Beaulieu Road, to the West Overcliff Drive.

It was here, while staying at Branksome Dene (now Zetland Court) in Alumhurst Road – the seaside residence of his aunt, Lady Wimborne – that Winston Spencer Churchill (1874-1965) nearly fell to his death on 10 January 1893. The 18-year-old leapt from the rustic bridge while playing a game of tag with his younger brother, Jack, and a cousin.

Winston intended grabbing a pine branch but misjudged the jump and bounced 29 feet to the ground. He suffered concussion and a ruptured kidney and had to convalesce for a couple of months. Branksome Dene Chine has also been claimed for the location of the misadventure but the description in Churchill's *My Early Life* best fits Alum Chine.

By January 1893, his Pacific adventure having taken him via Samoa, Robert Louis Stevenson was suffering a bout of influenza as well as the chronic lung congestion that had brought him to Bournemouth and its sanatorium culture. He continued working but broke off from *The Ebb-*

Hardly a glimpse from the same spot in 2008

On top in a view posted in 1957

Tide for a light-weight story called *St Ives* about a French prisoner escaping from Edinburgh in 1814.

Stevenson's Bournemouth home, which he called Skerryvore for the famous lighthouse designed by his engineer uncle, Alan Stevenson, was at 61 Alum Chine Road. It was damaged by a German bomb on 15 November 1940. No one troubled to repair it, and in 1954, after the rubble had been cleared, Bournemouth Corporation turned it into a memorial garden. The shape of the house footings is marked out with stone footings and flower beds. The centrepiece is a miniature Skerryvore lighthouse.

'No Cycling' in action, 2008

Bournemouth's shield of arms, above Middle Chine

WEST OVERCLIFF DRIVE

The mile-long project for West Overcliff Drive, extending from Durley Chine in the east to Alum Chine in the west was staked out on the ground early in 1901. Approval had been given by James Edward Cooper-Dean (1840-1921) of Littledown House who granted Bournemouth Corporation a 999-year lease of the cliff and chine slopes as well as the land for the scenic highway. He also rented two acres, for £50 per annum, which became the clifftop Argyll Pleasure Garden.

Work began at the West Cliff end and the new drive skirted the western edge of Durley Chine, before turning inland along the eastern side of Middle Chine. Then it crosses the upper section of this chine, on an ornamental iron bridge, into what is now McKinley Road. Here the drive turns immediately left, southwards, to follow the steep west bank of Middle Chine to the top of the cliff.

The next bend brings the drive to Alum Chine, the widest and longest of the three ravines, where it turns inland via a series of graceful curves. Below, just around the corner from the seaward end, is the Tropical Garden which is tucked away in its own microclimate. The road continues into Westbourne where it joins West Cliff Road beside St Ambrose Church. James Cooper-Dean donated the land for this new Anglican church in 1896.

Then the drive feeds into Alum Chine Road and brings us to the inland extremity of the chine woods beside the Alum-hurst Road roundabout.

The official handover of West Overcliff Drive, from landowner James Cooper-Dean to the Mayor, Dr George Frost was scheduled for 16 October 1902. In the event it was delayed until 6 November 1902.

No houses or trees in 1903

Trees hide the houses in 2008

11

MIDDLE CHINE

Middle Chine is Alum Chine writ small, with the same loss of exposed sand on the landward side of the promenade. Time-warp photographs, however, show it totally unchanged from the period when smuggling was the principal industry in these sparsely populated stretches of easily accessible coastline. Liquor, silk, and tea were the principal contraband from France.

Middle Chine, Bournemouth.

Posted in 1909

As close as you can get and still see something in 2008

THE SANDS, MIDDLE CHINE, BOURNEMOUTH

M.D. to Mrs Sampson, Trezelah, Gulval, near Penzance, on 7 June 1909: **'Mother and Aunt arrived home. Willie drove in for them. Aunt and I are going to the fair this afternoon. Mother looks well. Will keep cape until you come.'**

H. May to Miss K. Gunner, 65 Stafford Road, Norfolk Park, Sheffield, on 16 April 1907: **'Thanks so much for your letter about Alton. I did not go and look at it as I thought it did not sound suitable. I looked at Southsea & Lymington, but thought neither of them would do, so in the end we decided to stop here, for the 6 months, which will be up on the 5th of June, when I expect we shall go home. I hope you are quite well. The weather is getting brighter now. We brought some of our own bulbs for this little garden & they look so nice.'**

Elsie & Harold to Miss Webber, 28 Friarn Street, Bridgwater, Somerset, on 19 September 1908: **'Still having a jolly time. Going to Southampton tomorrow.'**

L. White to Miss Brooks, School House, Church Knowle, Dorset, on 1 October 1915: **'Just one for your collection. Hope you are well.'**

Arrival of a land train from the pier, 2008

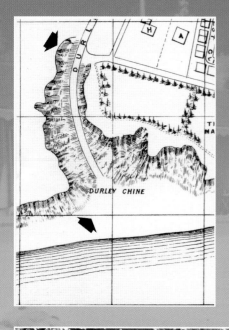

Parking in the mid-1930s

DURLEY CHINE

Before the building of the Undercliff Promenade, in 1912, the geological 'leaf beds' of Durley Chine – exposed in the cliff just above at head height – were famous for their Eocenean tropical flora sandwiched in a lenticular layer of lignitic clay. These riverborne freshwater deposits, characterised by pinkish clay above yellow sand, occurred intermittently between Bournemouth Pier and Canford Cliffs.

The name is a transferred one, from the Hampshire hamlet of Durley, near the Bishop's Waltham home of early 19th-century owner William Dean.

Durley Chine, because it was the closest to the town, soon became a car park for Bourne-

From the same spot in 2008

mouth's western coast. In fact it still is, and also has licensed premises, with the Durley Inn overlooking the beach. Seeing the cars, however, is another matter. They can now be secreted in the shade.

> Mary to Mrs F. Bath at 11 Kensington Gardens in Bath, circa 1908: 'A lovely day today. We have been on the sand all the morning & are going again later on. Too warm for a coat, almost. Myrtle thinks it's just grand here. We have almost 15 minutes walk to the sea.'
>
> Cutting from the *Western Mail*, Cardiff, in the 1930s: 'If the reader has not stood on Durley Chine and been enchanted by the sweep of sand and sea, stretching in its magnificent curve as far as the eye can reach, then there is one of the joys of life in store.'

The cars, however, have not gone away

Beach view before the promenade, in 1910

The sands in 2008, to high-rise Admiral's Walk, the Marriott Highcliff Hotel and the Albany

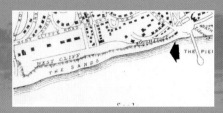

WEST CLIFF

Work on a western beach road and promenade began beside Bournemouth Pier in 1910. The Undercliff Promenade – delayed by the Great War and then years of economic crisis – did not link up with the far section at Durley Chine and Alum Chine until 1930. The clifftop is dominated by the Marriott Highcliff Hotel in St Michael's Road.

Across to West Cliff from the pier in 1930

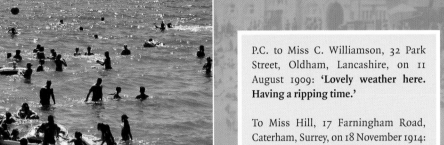

From the pier in 2008

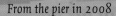

P.C. to Miss C. Williamson, 32 Park Street, Oldham, Lancashire, on 11 August 1909: **'Lovely weather here. Having a ripping time.'**

To Miss Hill, 17 Farningham Road, Caterham, Surrey, on 18 November 1914: **'We are having a glorious time. The weather is perfect. This is such a pretty place, such lovely walks, all heather and pines on the cliffs. It must be nice in the summer.'**

Ciss to Mrs Hillman, 25 Wilchmill Lane, Frome, Somerset, on 8 August 1922: **'Just a card to let you see I have not forgotten you. Having a delightful time. The weather is simply lovely now but it poured all day Sunday. Are you coming down for a day?'**

Faun to Mrs Read, Station House, Stonehouse, Gloucestershire, on 16 June, circa 1923: **'Arrived safely. Splendid journey. Very good to see Alf yesterday. Thunder last night. Beautiful today. Going around the Isle of Wight tomorrow by water.'**

L.V. to Miss M. A. Mellick, Springfield, Nailsea, near Bristol, on 1 October 1925: **'Am having very nice weather. Trust all is well and that your cold is quite gone. Shall be changing my address Saturday – will advise you later where I am going. Please lock up well on Saturday. Put all box files in steel cabinet.'**

The Highcliff Hotel which remains the dominant building, 1993

THE BEACH (Westwards)

Closer glimpses of the sands and cliffs below the Highcliffe Hotel (before it dropped the 'e' as the Swallow Highcliff Hotel and now the Marriott Highcliff Hotel) on the brow of the West Cliff, down through Beacon Road to South Cliff Road. The five-storey Highcliffe boasted 'approximately 500 feet of sea frontage'. This was and is the western heart of our holiday coast. The lower block of four-storey buildings is the far end of Solent Cliffs Hotel which catered for 130 guests and had 'two full-sized billiards tables by Thurstons free to visitors'. Behind, distinctive with rounded bay windows, was the two-storey Meyrick Cliffs Hotel.

Four-storey buildings along the top included the Beacon Royal Hotel and Charborough Hall Hotel which was named for Charborough House because of its Drax family connections. Overlooking the pier were Berkeley Hall Hotel and Brownswood Hall on South Cliff and the Court Royal down towards Exeter Road.

The 1922 view is before the building on the left-hand side of the West Cliff Lift below the dome-topped six-storey Tollard Royal Hotel. This advertised an American bar and a 'Vita-glass sun lounge flooded every evening and on dull days with health-giving ultra violet rays'. Its most notorious guest was the debonair double murderer Neville Heath whose novel way of avoiding attention was to style himself in the register as 'Group Captain Rupert Brooke'. He was hanged on 26 October 1946.

The West Cliff Zig-Zag was opened on 1 April 1985 during the mayorship of Councillor M. H. Filer and Beach and Cliffs Committee chairman Councillor W. F. Forman. Shelters below the cliff have evolved into attractions from amusement arcades to the Oceanarium. Above a strip of green, the profile of South Cliff since the 1980s has been the warm red lines of the BIC – Bournemouth International Centre – with its Olympic-sized baths as well as one of the biggest

Crown seal on a manhole cover beside the BIC, 1999

Before provision of the cliff lift (left side) in a view posted in 1922

After the lift and before the war, in 1938

Beach-huts and Happyland amusements along to Westover Rowing Club, 2008

Highcliff Hotel to the BIC from further seaward, 2008

conference halls in the country. This has seen a succession of national political conferences with speeches by Prime Ministers Thatcher, Major, Blair and Brown.

They were not always right in their reading of events, such as in this forecast relayed from the BIC by Trevor Kavanagh for *The Sun* on 11 October 1986: **'Maggie Thatcher predicted that the Tories would stay in power until the next century in a fighting speech which won her a massive standing ovation on the last day of the party conference in Bournemouth yesterday.'**

For signs of security in an age of terrorism, look up for police marksmen, or down to find that the manholes have been checked and sealed, or seawards for the marine patrol.

Cecil to Miss Norah Wade, Mia Mia, Dunsfold, near Godalming, Surrey, on 11 August 1905: **'I haven't forgotten to send you a card this time.'**

U.C. to Mrs Collings in Hoddesdon, Hertfordshire, on New Year's Day in 1909: **'We've been having frightful weather, & wishing ourselves back home again.'**

Lewis to Miss Nellie Tillson, 48 Hillier Road, Wandsworth Common, on 23 February 1927: **'We are still having rather unsettled weather here but the change has made me so much stronger. We should like to see the sun more often! Hope you enjoyed the fog last week!'**

Harry to Florence and Tom in Balsall Heath, Birmingham, on a June day in the reign of George V: **'We are having a lovely time and the weather is perfect.'**

Bournemouth International Centre and the Oceanarium, 2008

South Cliff steps and the view across the pier to a battleship in the bay, 1906

Calm before the political storm, 1939

PIER APPROACH

This was the Bourne Mouth of the first Ordnance Survey map, in 1811, when there were no buildings and the Bourne Stream flowed across the beach. It comes from four miles inland, from Bourne Bottom, which is between Loewy Crescent and St Brelades Avenue at Alderney.

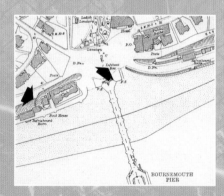

South Cliff steps and the view across the beach, 2008

From further along South Cliff, 2008

Development at Pier Approach revealed the saturated timber and roots of a subterranean forest. The trees, identified as Scots pine, had been inundated when sea levels rose as the world warmed in about 12000 BC. Coincidentally, three million saplings of the same species were planted across the Bournemouth plateau, between 1810 and 1820.

The clock in the entrance tower at Pier Approach was presented to the town in 1882 by Horace Davy MP whose Christchurch constituency included the new town of Bournemouth. Beach shows around the pier included Birchmore & Lindon's Pierrots and the Gay Cadets.

The first Corporation Baths dated from 1864 and were replaced on the same site by the new Corporation Baths. Site clearance started in 1934, with the foundation stone for the replacement baths being laid by the Mayor, Alderman John Robert Edgecombe on 6 November 1935. The opening took place on 23 March 1937 and was carried out by a civil servant, R. S. Hudson, from the Ministry of Health.

To quote from *Bournemouth, Britain's All-Seasons Resort, Official Guide for 1939-40* :

'Bournemouth is fortunate in the possession of a six-mile bathing beach which is unrivalled in Britain, and the new Baths give equally outstanding facilities for indoor bathing. They have entailed an expenditure of nearly £80,000. The main part of the suite is occupied by the swimming pool, its dimensions being 100 ft. by 35 ft. Special attention has been given to ensure a perfect sterile water supply to the pool, and frequent samples are taken and examined by a bacteriologist. The 150,000 gallon

Win & Bert to Mrs J. H. Frayne, 30 Greenbank Avenue, Plymouth, on 10 August 1931: **'We are now at Poole, seeing the sights, and dodging the showers. Hope all at home are alright. Somebody sent us two P.C.'s. [postcards] this morning from Plymouth. So cheerio until tomorrow night.'**

Granda to Miss Margaret Tyler, 49 Welsford Avenue, Devonport, on 27 May 1940: **'I was ever so pleased to receive your card this morning. You will be surprised to hear that I went to church twice yesterday, in the morning by myself, and in evening Mr and Mrs H. and visitors, 7 in all. Church crowded. I don't know why, but I have not had my usual weather, rain all Sunday morning, but fine rest of day. Able to sit in deck-chair on front in the afternoon. I am OK. Heaps of love.'**

Daughter to Mrs W. M. Edge, Wood Street, Mansfield, Nottinghamshire, on 13 March 1904: '**Hope you received the letter this morning. We were caught in a hail-storm this morning and it is fearfully cold. Dada is getting on nicely so far, but he cannot get out much.**'

Lillie M. J. Powell to Miss R. Harding, 42 Kempshott Road, Streatham, London SW, on 21 August 1904: '**I see in the *Girls Realm* that Miss Harding wishes to exchange P.P.C.s** [picture postcards]. **I shall have much pleasure in exchanging with her, for views of London (good ones) in return, views of Bournemouth & vicinity.**'

Aunt M. to Miss Ethel Kelsey, 15 Olive Street, Hartlepool, on 5 May 1906: '**As promised I send you some P.C. of this lovely place. We are having glorious weather. Sorry not to have seen your people before I left. Will be home on Monday midnight.**'

F.C. to Miss Olive Beale, 39 Clarendon Road, Walthamstow, on 17 July 1906: '**Hope you are much better. I shall be in Walthamstow on 3rd August for about a week or 10 days. Then I am going to Caterham to my old place. Give my love to your Mother. Hope I shall see you all soon.**'

Annie to Miss Minnie Lunbreck, King Street, Dawlish, on 8 August 1908: '**Have had a ripping week. Am going to sail to Poole today but return home on Monday. Hope you have enjoyed yourself. In haste.**'

Showering, 1999

contents of the pool are circulated so as to ensure a complete change of water every four hours. The Bath is fitted with diving equipment to the latest requirements of the Amateur Diving Association, and aquatic displays, swimming trials, galas, and similar events, are regular features. The pool is surrounded by terraced seating accommodation for over 600 spectators. In addition to the swimming pool, the Baths are also equipped for providing Turkish and a variety of private baths, including Pine Essence, Brine, Foam, Douche, and Sea Water.'

Swimming has now moved across the slope into Bournemouth International Centre. The Baths site has been redeveloped as the Waterfront complex which includes an Imax cinema. Up the hill, the prominent buildings with a view over the Pier Approach are the Odeon Centre and former Palace Court Hotel. There, in the mid-1930s, waiter Robert Dashwood's most appreciative regular customers were the Prince of Wales and Mrs Simpson who, he recalled, generally chose between grilled fillet steak and Dover sole and always tipped generously.

Carts, cars, and the new Corporation Baths, 1938

Flats, tattoo parlour and the new Waterfront Imax, 2008

BOURNEMOUTH PIER

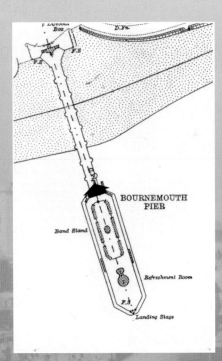

A jetty was built here in 1855. It was replaced by the first Bournemouth Pier, described as 'handsome and adequate', which opened on 17 September 1861. Ship-worms soon found its timber piles and these weaknesses were tested to destruction in a gale on 5 January 1867:

> **'High on the beach it was thrown like a stranded wreck on a sandbank; tall piles wrested in twain, and iron twisted like pack-thread, covered the yellow strand of the sun-loving village of Bournemouth.'**

Eugenius Birch, grand-master of Victorian pier-building, was commissioned to build the replacement Bournemouth Pier. Florence Newlyn laid the foundation stone on 9 November 1878. The Birch pier was iron-framed, 838 feet long and 35 feet wide along its main span, which widened at the seaward end into a canopied pier head, 110 feet wide. There were pavilions and promenades, elegant abutments, a bandstand, and galleries for the steamers to disgorge the masses who had newly popularised the seaside. It was opened by Sir Francis Wyatt Truscott, the Lord Mayor of London, on 11 August 1880.

'Please keep to the right' in a view across to the East Cliff, 1904

Towards the Swimming Baths and beach shelters in 1906

Towards South Cliff and Exeter Road in a view posted in 1906

The Bournemouth, Swanage, & Poole Steamboat Co. operated from the pier with paddle-steamers *Lord Elgin* (1881), *Brodick Castle* (1887) and *Windsor Castle* (1891). A landing stage extension to the pier was opened by the Lord Mayor of London, Sir George Wyatt Truscott – Sir Francis Truscott's son – on 5 June 1909.

Militarisation of Bournemouth seafront took place in June 1940 as the threat of German invasion followed the Fall of France. As well constructing obstacles with barbed-wire, gun emplacements, mines and tank-traps, Royal Engineer demolition teams blew-up the central sections of this and other South Coast piers.

The far end remained as an island until John Mowlem & Co. Ltd of London – the construction company founded by a Swanage stone merchant – rebuilt the pier in the mid-1950s. The Pier Theatre opened in 1960. Over the years, however, all other embellishments have been removed – even the ornate lamps – leaving only the basic cast-iron frame from the Eugenius Birch original.

White-out on the boards, 25 April 1908

Even that has come under threat. Just before closing time on Thursday 12 August 1993, when headlines in the Irish Troubles moved across the water to British targets, a Provisional IRA active service unit left six incendiary bombs in Bournemouth stores. Then, after dark, they scaled the underside of Bournemouth Pier with two explosive devices packed in black bin-liners. The small one was planted beneath the western walkway and a 'substantial' one attached to stanchions below the Pier Theatre. The first exploded at 04.33 hours on 13 August but the main bomb failed to detonate, being found at 08.30, after which it was defused and

To Mr F. J. Parkyn, Cleeve Road, Knowle, Bristol, on 24 July 1906: **'Thanks for Photo. Not at all bad considering conditions of weather & people. Look here, no insult, our programme is as under – 6.30 wake up. 7.0 or at latest 7.15 get out of bed. 8.0 breakfast & read funny letters. 8.30 shopping. 9.0 walk to Boscombe by road and paddle back, 2 miles in the water. 1 o'clock dinner. 1.30 still at it. 2 o'clock very tired. To be continued.'**

Nobbs to Miss E. Stone, King Street, Stroud, Gloucestershire, on 26 August 1907: **'Oh what we're seeing. weather is simply grand. Going to Cherbourg on Monday.'**

Bess to Miss Nell Jones, Queen Camel, near Yeovil, on 10 September 1907: **'Many thanks for P.C. I was so pleased to get it. I shall be glad to get a letter from you. Then I will write one to you. i had a very good time last Sunday. I will tell you all when I write . . . This is where I hope to go tomorrow. There are going to be some sports there.'**

F.J.K. to Mr G. H. Brown, 4 Damer's Road, Dorchester, on 28 August, in the reign of George V: **'We are having a splendid time. The weather has behaved itself properly. Sorry we are not here for another week.'**

Edith to Mr Halliday, 105 West Street, Boston, Lincolnshire, from Southampton on 1 September 1920: **'Dear Dad, Thought you would like view of pier. Went to Bournemouth by road yesterday. 15 of us. It was hot on the sands.'**

Margaret to Mr & Mrs Tyler, 49 Welsford Avenue, Stoke, Devonport, on 17 August 1939: **'We are sitting in the pier waiting for the band to start. It's boiling here. The train gets in at Plymouth 8.10 p.m. Till then cheerio.'**

Turnstile down to the steamers, with Victoria being advertised in 1909

removed. Meanwhile, in the early hours, the fire-bombs in the town centre shops had caused considerable damage, though sprinklers and firemen saved the buildings.

The biggest excitement these days, apart from *The Magic of Laughter* in the Pier Theatre, is a speedboat ride. *Shockwave* offers '900 horsepower of raw adrenaline' at £7.50 a ticket, from the same point that the paddle steamers came and went in a more sedate age.

Promenading past the same point in 1910

Checking the boat times (right) in a view posted in 1912

Shockwave pulling away from the lower deck, 2008

The steps down to the boats, 2008

Walking the boards in 2008

THE BEACH
(Eastwards)

Seen from the pier, paddling and boating in 1908

Beach licences in 1900 were restricted to:

- 2 parties of vocalists (such as the black and white minstrels).
- 1 punch and judy show.
- 2 ice-cream stalls (one being C. Capocci from Italy).
- 4 photographers (only two at a time on either side of the pier).
- 2 kinestoscopes (or similar apparatus).
- 1 temperance refreshment tent (though only at bank holiday and regatta days.

Bathing was segregated with males and females being separated by a strip of clear, blue water. It was an offence to come within 20 yards of an area reserved for the opposite gender. As for the females, bye-laws required that they were suitably clad:

'Ladies shall wear a tunic, or blouse, reaching from the neck to the knees, with belt and knickerbocker drawers.'

West of Durley Chine and beyond Boscombe Chine, swimming was permitted without use of a bathing machine, but only between 7.00 am and 1.00 p.m. The end of Bournemouth Pier was available for plunge diving but only from 5.00 am to 7.00 am:

'During the early hours of the morning bathing may be indulged in from the end of the Pier. A springboard is attached for the convenience of bathers who may enjoy the luxury of a dip in the briny where the water is deep and clear.'

Though required to avoid 'immodest exposure' and the areas reserved for females, males were otherwise permitted to splash about at will, provided they came and went via a bathing machine.

Groyne close-up, sunday 27 july 2008

Seen from the pier, paddling without boats, 2008

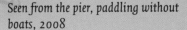

Miss Parrott for Mrs Bascombe of Cassiobury, Glen Road, Boscombe, to Bournemouth & District Laundry, Avon Road, Bournemouth, on 13 August 1907: '**1 pair child's combinations not enclosed in laundry parcel. Kindly forward at once.**'

A.L. to Mrs Edwards, Bee-Hive Hotel, Cheltenham, on 13 April 1912: '**Dear Aunt, I daresay mother has told you we are here for 2 or 3 months. It is lovely here & we are having a nice time. Hope Uncle and yourself are well.**'

'L' to Ernest Nightingale at Holly Lodge, Knockholt, Kent, on arrival by paddle-steamer, 10 June 1912: '**We are over here today. Weather glorious. Had a lovely crossing & lunch on the beach. Wish you were here.**'

G. Fish to Miss Pike, High Street, Stour Provost, Dorset, on 8 August 1921: '**I am out of hospital and doing well. Staying here for fortnight. It is lovely. Go on the beach every day.**'

Cars and changing booths, looking down from East Cliff path, 1933

Land train and the beach from East Cliff path, 2008

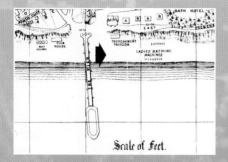

Scale of Feet.

EAST CLIFF

The Undercliff Drive and Promenade began from the Pier in 1906 and reached the partly-built East Cliff Lift in the autumn of 1907. A century later, the near view has hardly changed, except for the disappearance of beach shows and rowing boats. In fact, despite predictions of a rising sea level, no one seems to have told the English Channel and if anything there is more sand.

That defies the doom and gloom prophesies of late Victorian times, stirred in particular by bearded lobbyist and publicist Joseph Cutler who built Boscobel Tower on the Flagpole site at Terrace Mount, South Cliff, in the early 1880s. Contemplation on the state of the beach persuaded him it would be washed away once the sea wall was built. There were times when it seemed he might be right, but the control of tidal drift by a series of groynes has done as well as anyone could have envisaged, apart perhaps from the marine engineers who built them. Waves regularly crashing over the promenade has become a distant memory. For a time, however, it seemed that Cutler might be right and Bournemouth's sand would all end up on Studland beach.

Along the top of the East Cliff the principal visual change has been the rise – and continuing rise – of the tower block. Biggest and tallest is the gleaming white Albany in Manor Road. Ironically, as they fell out of favour in cities and the suburbs, rooms with a view became de rigueur on the seaside. The difference is that here they come with lifts, janitors and security.

On a warm July Sunday in 2008

Damp day, in a view beside the new Undercliff Drive, posted in 1908

87 - View from Bournemouth Pier looking East

Elsie to Miss M. Mellick, Brookwood, Edgcumbe Road, Redland, Bristol, on 13 April 1903: '**Walks. We went to a place called Boscombe, Friday & also to another place called Poole, Friday. We went on the Golf Links Saturday. Sunday we went to a place called Branksome, through Talbot Woods, & across Meyrick Park. This morning we went to a place called Christchurch., where there is a very fine church & castle. We are coming home Wed. or Thurs.**'

Sent from Teignmouth, to Mrs Batten, Battenberg, Ashburton, Devon on an Edwardian card which has had its stamp steamed off: '**Wishing you both a very happy Xmas & New Year. When are you coming to see us? Have been staying with friends in Bournemouth & quite enjoyed it. Have had a cold since my return but am better.**'

Hot day, with the Dominoes performing, in a view posted in 1909

Celebratory crowds for the arrival of Bournemouth's charter of incorporation, dispatched by rail from Privy Council, 27 August 1890

East Cliff path and bathing machines in a view posted in 1906

EAST CLIFF

The arrival of the tower blocks – first Palace Court Hotel and then Bath Hill Court in 1935 – brought a new dimension to the Bournemouth skyline. 'Location, location, location,' was the maxim coined by Lord Samuel of Land Securities. These shots show the growth and re-growth of one such hot spot since 1880. A particular pinch-point remains in limbo where Kildare was the second villa down the hill from the Royal Bath Hotel. It was there where Fabian socialist Beatrice Potter – the future Mrs Sidney Webb – lodged with her father for three winters from 1885 to 1888. Leigh Hatts, the historian, links it to visits from T. H. Huxley and Herbert Spencer. The site is a car-park.

Shelters and the new promenade on a busy day in 1908

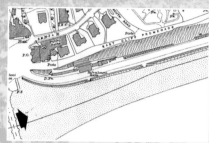

The skyline fills, with Palace Court Hotel (top left) and Bath Hill Court rising to the right, in 1935

(Bottom left) Further along East Cliff, the Carlton Hotel (towards the top right) was almost alone in peeking over the top, in 1935

(Bottom right) The near view on Sunday 27 July 2008

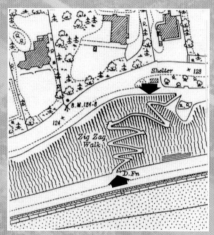

Looking up, in a view posted in 1909

Red zone – for cycles and dogs

EAST CLIFF ZIG-ZAG

Big Chine, as it was originally called, became known for a short while as Steps Chine when residents and visitors began using the sandy hollow as a direct route to the beach. The other route down, towards Boscombe, was Toft Steps. In 1908 the crumbling hollow at Big Chine was embraced by the emerging municipality and suburbanised as 'East Cliff Zig-Zag Path' to link Meyrick Road and Lansdowne district with the sea.

The path here drops from 125 feet (38 metres) above sea level to that of the Undercliff Drive which is – or should be – 10 feet (3 metres) above the water-line.

Retaining walls were built in Purbeck stone and bamboo planted to stabilise the cliffs which formerly teemed with sand lizards. The first national record for the smooth snake, their principal predator, came from near the flagstaff down by the beach, caught by a Bournemouth resident and sent to the British Museum by the Honourable Alfred Russell in 1859. Lizards, at least, are still present today.

The Zig-Zag itself comprises eight inclines, each 7 feet wide, with recesses for seats beside each of the corners. As with so much of the western and central seafront, this sandy gash has scrubbed-up to the point of obstructing photography, though the impenetrable bamboo plantation of my childhood looks as if it has been eaten and trampled by a collective noun of pandas. Pink-flowering and fleshy Hottentot fig, purple maritime tree mallow, and lush tall Alexanders are taking its place. Something of the natural fauna clings on, however, to the extent that signs proclaim the rights of the endangered sand lizard.

Looking down, in a view posted in 1913

Looking down in 2008

Looking up in 2008

CLIFF LIFTS

Bournemouth's famous golden sands were fed by a constant succession of cliff collapses. That dynamic process was not compatible with building on the Overcliff. For years, progressive pressure demanded sea defences along the Undercliff but traditionalists fought to retain the natural look. The most powerful positive argument came from Sir Joseph Bazalgette (1819-91), engineer of the London Sanitary Authority, who had created the Thames Embankment.

Opening day on 6 November 1907 (spot the crowd on top)

Construction of East Cliff Lift in 1907

From the Undercliff Drive before the Great War

Looking up in 2008

The go-ahead for the project was given to Bournemouth Corporation by landowner Sir George Meyrick in March 1903 but he imposed a ten-year timetable. A seven-man team was sent off to study sea defences around the North Sea from Scarborough to Scheveningen. The Undercliff Drive Deputation reported in November 1903.

Costing £59,200, work on the promenade began in January 1907, together with excavation and construction of East Cliff Lift below Meyrick Road, on a direct pedestrian route from the Lansdowne. The Undercliff Drive and Promenade were built to this point from the Pier Approach and opened by Mayor John Aldridge Parsons on 6 November 1907.

The electronically powered cable-operated Swiss style funicular railway was completed in 1908. Its upper platform, set into the clifftop plateau, is at about 110 feet above the water. Down at 10 feet above sea-level, the extension of the beach road eastwards to Boscombe Pier was declared open by the Earl and Countess of Malmesbury, from Hurn Court, on 3 June 1914. As with Mayor Parsons and the 1907 ribbon-cutting the location was chosen for the very accessibility that the lift provided.

Bureaucrats and builders had just about coped with Sir George Meyrick's deadline. Meanwhile an era was drawing to its close as the glorious summer gave way to war across both Europe and the globe.

Two random thoughts occur. Although the concept is hardly green, the pricing qualifies in that £1.10 for the journey up in 2008, compared with 70p for going down, reflects the disparity

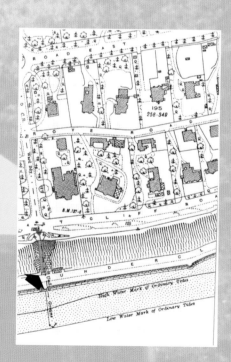

in the energy required. On the other hand, I recall being told that cabin on one side was used for going up, and the other reserved for coming down. This still sounds quite logical but on reflection it could only work once. I was being teased.

To Mrs Oliver at South Views, Alcester, near Shaftesbury, on 12 February 1909: **'Dear Mother, Just a card to thank you for your letter. This is the lift. How would you like to go up it?'**

Lydia to Miss L. Eldridge at Little Forest House in Cliff Road, Bournemouth, on 1 February 1913: **'Thanks for P.C. this morning. Sorry you could not come today. I think we could meet you on the cliffs by the seat at the top of hill by Bath Hotel tomorrow at 3.15 p.m.'**

Sid to Master Frank Edmonds in St Sampsons, Guernsey, dated 19 July in the reign of George V: **'You ought to be here to see the Punch and Judy shows and games on the sands. In Bournemouth there are lifts just like trams which go up the cliff. This afternoon I am going to the station to see the trains pass, some with two engines. There is one big engine, called the baby engine, about 150 tons. 112 trams in Poole.'**

Looking down in 2008

SEAFRONT TARIFF 2008

CLIFF LIFTS

	Down	Up
Adult	£0.70	£1.10
Junior *(U-16)*	£0.50	£0.70
Freestyle Card	£0.50	£0.70
Family *(up to 2 Adults & 3 Juniors)*	£2.20 SAVE 70p	£3.20 SAVE £1.10

Under 5's and **permanent wheelchair users** (plus 1 carer) enjoy **free travel** on Cliff Lifts and Land Trains as well as exemption from Pier Tolls. *Ask inside for further details...*

BEACH EQUIPMENT HIRE

	Daily Hire 9am - 6pm	After 3pm
Deck Chairs	£2.00	£1.00
Freestyle Card Holder		
Deck Chair	£1.50	£1.00
Sunbeds	£4.00	£2.00
Windbreaks	£2.00	£1.00
Parasols	£4.00	

recycle for Bournemouth

Help us to keep our award winning beaches clean by using the blue bins for food and general waste and recycling bins for plastic, metal and glass. Please do not leave litter on the beach.

KEEP BOURNEMOUTH SEAFRONT TIDY

☎ 01202 451781
www.bournemouth.gov.uk/visitors/seafront

Bournemouth Seafront

Beach-huts beside Undercliff Drive, 1999

Current tariff, 2008

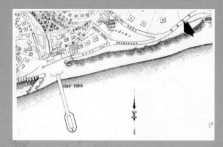

The pier from the cliffs in a view before building of the Undercliff Drive, posted in 1903

Ethel to Miss A. Jeffery in Shipton Moyne, near Tetbury, Gloucestershire, on 12 June 1905: 'Walt, Hilda & I are down here for the day. It is simply lovely, the weather lovely. We have been sitting on the sands . . . Must tell all news when I see you.'

Fred to Miss E. long, 6 Westbourne Road, Trowbridge, on 28 July 1915: 'What delightful weather I am having. Just a few little showers to-day. Went to Christchurch by train & back by tram yesterday. Have been to The Haven, Sandbanks, to-day.'

F. C. White to Miss Jennings at the Rectory, Paglesham, Essex, on 1 June 1932: 'If you have any farthing boxes, will you kindly bring them to the "All Day" tomorrow, in case they are wanted.'

Autumn lights, from East Cliff Zig-Zag, seen with artistic licence in 1932

The pier from the closest cliffside exposure, 2008

The pier from East Cliff path, 2008

Millennium sunset in autumn 2000

The beach at 3.15 on the Pier Approach clock, Sunday 27 July 2008

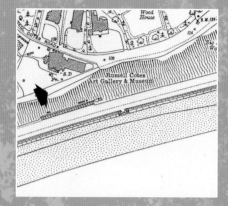

Inside view, 1925

EAST CLIFF HALL

On 6 November 1907, Merton and Annie Russell-Cotes announced that they were giving East Cliff Hall to the town, along with its art collection and eclectic contents, for a museum. The date was chosen to coincide with the opening that day of the first section of the Undercliff Drive, which passed below their home, in a project which Russell-Cotes had been advocating for decades. The following year the couple were made honorary freemen of the borough and in 1909 King Edward VII capped it by bestowing the honour of knighthood upon Merton Russell-Cotes.

House and grounds, 1912

From the East Cliff path, 1913

Now only glimpsed from the path

The view from the grounds, 2008

Born at Tettenham, near Wolverhampton, in 1835, Merton Russell-Cotes travelled the world and made his fortune in Irish life assurance. He came to Bournemouth in 1876, buying the Bath Hotel and setting about persuading the London and South Western Railway to bring a direct line across the New Forest, from Brockenhurst.

East Cliff Hall was designed in the style of an Italian Riviera villa by architect John Frederick Fogerty in 1894.

Its hand-over to the Borough of Bournemouth took place in stages. The official date, on the plaque on the wall, is given as 15 July 1916. Lady Russell-Cotes died in 1920 and Sir Merton on 27 January 1921. The entire hall then became the Russell-Cotes Art Gallery and Museum. Part had already been opened to the public, by Princess Beatrice – youngest daughter of Queen Victoria – on the couple's 59th wedding anniversary in 1919. There is also a museum inside a museum in the form of a room devoted to the famous actor Sir Henry Irving (1838-1905) who was among their closest friends.

1916 museum dedication plaque, 2008

The post-war Carlton Hotel, in a view posted in 1946

The Carlton Hotel in 2008

CARLTON HOTEL

Victorian boarding houses eastwards along the cliffs from Brumstath were merged into a single building, connected by corridors and extensions, to become one of Britain's grand hotels. The inaugural dinner for the directors and their friends took place in September 1903.

This was the first Bournemouth establishment to come into a category that we would recognise as luxury hotel. It was, however, firmly from another age in that it did not encourage night life (or dogs):

> **'Electric Light in Bedrooms – Electric light will be charged if used for other than ordinary purposes. Dogs cannot be catered for. The Lights are turned off in the Public Rooms at 11 p.m.'**

Fires in bedrooms or sitting rooms were extra, at a shilling for the morning or evening, one shilling and sixpence for the afternoon and evening, or two shillings for all day. The tariff for dinner, between 7.00 and 8.00 p.m., was five shillings for 'Soup, Fish, Entrees, Joints, Poultry or Game, Sweets with Dessert.' There was a proviso: 'Dogs cannot be provided for.'

Its Five-Star rating almost goes without saying since 1934. The Carlton enjoyed a good war and hosted General Dwight D. Eisenhower and General Sir Bernard Montgomery in the spring of 1944 as they planned the invasion of Europe. Meanwhile D-Day rehearsals took place in the bay and across Studland Heath. The luxurious Eden Suite dates from 1955 when Sir Anthony and Lady Eden came to town for the Conservative Party Conference.

Outwardly a bastion of patriotism, and often inwardly a bulwark of western values as it hosted major meetings of the North Atlantic Treaty Organisation, the Carlton Hotel set a cosmopolitan example in the 1950s. It became the practice to fly the national flags of visiting ambassadors and ministers beside the entrance. The hotel made headlines with the Hammer and Sickle – a case of the red flag flying here – such as 'Communist Flag flies over True Blue Carlton'. There were far more objections when it was the Rising Sun which revived raw memories of wartime Japanese atrocities. Red flags these days are those of Menzies Hotels.

History in the making with Eisenhower and Montgomery planning D-Day

The *Bournemouth Graphic* in 1903: 'The Carlton is luxury itself. Entering through a stately portico, a smartly-dressed page ushers the visitor into the great hall, where he at once realises the comfort and stateliness of the establishment. Here, guests are enjoying their morning weed [smoke] and paper, or chatting over the events of the day, comfortably ensconced in the easiest of chairs and evidently revelling in their surroundings. The whole of the woodwork is of fumed oak, even to the picture frames and general fitments. The hall and lounges are covered with rich Turkey carpets, and there is an abundance of couches, settees, and easy chairs, much of the furniture being Sheraton style with rich coverings of yellow and green silk. In the drawing room, in its arrangement, cosiness as well as elegance has been studied, with the result that an air of comfort, rather than oppressive grandeur, pervades it.'

'B' to Mrs D. P. Harper in Cowbridge Road, Cardiff, on 28 July 1948: '**Delightful weather.** Thoroughly enjoying doing nothing, even too hot to do much! Fond love.'

The entrance, 2008

Entrance and five-star logo, 2000

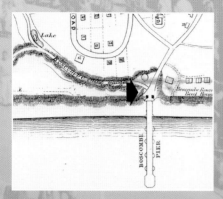

BOSCOMBE PIER

Boscombe Pier symbolised the aspirations of the new spa to be a budding equal to Bournemouth. Public meetings were held in 1885, an application made to the Board of Trade in 1886, and approval given in 1887. Two powerful men controlled Boscombe and its destiny.

The chairman of Boscombe Pier Company was Sir Henry Drummond Wolff and the principal shareholder was Sir Percy Shelley, the poet's only surviving son. The engineer was Archibald Smith of Southbourne, the builders Messrs. E. Howell of Poole, with ironwork from their Waterloo Foundry. The contract price was £3,813, plus £938 for making the pier approach, which was contracted out to James Edwards

Lady Jane Shelley, the wife of Sir Percy Florence Shelley (1819-89) of Boscombe Manor, pulled a lever which released the first pitch-pine pile on 17 October 1888. It was rammed by a steam hammer into the seabed. The length was 600 feet, by 32 feet wide, with shelters 'placed at intervals of 80 feet'. The Duke of Argyll cut a ribbon to declare the pier open on 29 July 1889.

For several years its special attraction was the 'Boscombe Whale' – a 65-feet skeleton – which was re-assembled on the pier after having been washed ashore below Portman Ravine on 7 January 1897.

The pier was 'Broken', in June 1940, to prevent it being used by the enemy if the Wehrmacht should arrive. It was still in a shambolic state more than ten years after the war had been over, with a only a jetty being reinstated, and full rebuilding was not completed until 1960. Even now it is a symbolic structure rather than a functional one. No amusements, no boating, and no pavilion. Sea-fishing is about the only activity.

'H.J.' to Miss Telly Hooper, 109 City Road, Bristol, 13 March 1921: '**Thanks for your letter.** I was sorry to hear you had a bad cold. I hope it's better by this time. We have had some lovely weather, but today it's changed, raining hard. I am still here. Our couple leaves tomorrow, so I shall be a general again as there is no work on board. I was hoping to be home for Easter. Alas, no luck. Reg is working for his brother, in Town, constant. There are hundreds out of work. Well dear, "be good".'

Unsigned, to Miss Annie Rowe in Rusthall, Tunbridge, on 26 September 1929: 'You will think me unkind not writing before but here we are and having a lovely time, with Olive and George, and our dear little Jean, and we are all fine. Shall be pleased to hear from you. I am going home tomorrow to my two lads, and I expect they will be glad to see me.'

German-printed early postcard of Boscombe Pier, 1900

The scene in 1910

BOSCOMBE PIER & BEACH.   0142

N&E. Marston
Boscombe.

Brilliant surfing conditions in 1922

'Auntie Vi and Uncle Arth' to Miss M. Tyler at 18 Treyew Road, Truro, on 12 August 1941: **'Here we are again at the same spot having a nice restful time.'** [This cannot have been the case in the literal sense as the pier-end featured in the card was now an island. It had also been mined. The access walkway was blown up by Royal Engineers in June 1940 to prevent its use by German invaders.]

Tent city in about 1925

Pier head with flag-day
hordes in the mid-1920s

Pier head in 2008

Pier head with a land train on the promenade in 2008

Treading the boards in 2008

Boscombe Pier in 2008

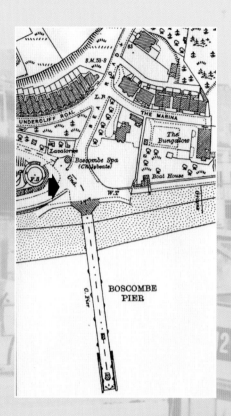

Bus arrival in a card posted in 1933

BOSCOMBE PIER APPROACH

The Undercliff Drive from East Cliff Lift to Sea Road, Boscombe, was completed in 1914. Above it, the Sandhill was ascended by a zig-zag path and under-cut by stone-built Shelters, though it otherwise remained wild and wind-blown.

Plots around the new Boscombe Spa were being sold from 1877 but the take-up was slow until May 1889 with the hiring of a special train from London and a marquee on the East Cliff to entice 'local and London capitalists'. Potential speculators viewed progress on Boscombe Pier, and pledged between £250 and £350 to reserve their chosen plot, before being taken by carriage to the Central Station for the seven o'clock train.

B.K.R. to Mr S. Rich, 27 Grosvenor Place, London SW, 11 October 1907: **'Fearfully rough again to-day. Can hardly walk on the cliffs. We are still having a glorious time. Have been drenched twice to-day.'**

Update from B.K.R. to Mr S. Rich, 12 October 1907: **'Still having a ripping time. Have all been to the Boscombe Hippodrome. Hope to hear from you soon.'**

Glad and George to Mrs & Mr Shettle, 27 Bonamy Street, Bermondsey, on 10 August 1927: **'We are having a fine time, weather grand. Doris is living in the water. We are spending the day at Christchurch. Hope you both feel better for your holiday.'**

Gladys and Billie to Granny Pike in the High Street, Stour Provost, Dorset, 4 August 1933: **'We are having a great time here. The weather until now has been good and if it lasts for another week it will be perfect. We hope that you are enjoying better health, also Nell, and hope that May is quite OK.'**

Steps down from the Sandhill, across to flats with the crane showing more to come, 2008

BOSCOMBE CHINE

The only facility here used to be a single ramshackle shelter. The Earl of Malmesbury promoted a scheme for a picturesque village to be called Boscombe Spa in 1866 but the initiative was seized by international diplomat Sir Henry Drummond Wolff (1830-1908). He bought what was described as 'a sandbank' of 23 acres, on a plateau 90 feet above sea-level, and set about creating 'a seaside Eden'. First he built Boscombe Towers, as his home, in 1868. Work started on Boscombe Spa Hotel in June 1872. Overlooking the chine and the sea it opened to the approval of the *Morning Post* on 1 September 1874:

> **'A new watering place has been started, a new place of refuge opened to the tired Londoner.'**

Known locally as 'the Great Improver', Drummond Wolff was the Member of Parliament for Christchurch – which included Bournemouth – and renowned in the wider world as a conservative guru. He led an influential clique known as 'The Owls' (Owls Road was named for these thinking Tories), and hosted the conference at which the Primrose League was founded. That flower was Disraeli's favourite though it became linked to Prince Albert after an ambiguous remark by Queen Victoria. Boscombe Spa Hotel briefly became Bournemouth College, in 1880, but reopened as Boscombe Chine Hotel in October 1885. It continues as the Chine Hotel, 25 Boscombe Spa Road.

The main western chine at Boscombe is a wet one, with a stream, which used to widen into a children's paddling pool. There is a bog garden for wildlife. This makes a colourful splash with hostas, *Primula japonica* hybrids, and the white-stemmed oriental bramble *Robus cockburnianus*.

Described as 'dark, gloomy and oppressive' after a murder and a suicide there in July 1995, the gardens were partially opened up both physically and visually. Heathland slopes have been

Revd. Francis Kilvert visited here in December 1875, though the relevant volume of his diaries was destroyed, and we have only a recollection of: '. . . wild sad sweet trysts in the snow and under pine trees, among the sand hills on the East Cliff and in Boscombe Chine.'

'L.C.' to Miss I. Eldridge, Davenport Cottages, Surrey Road, Bournemouth, on 11 April 1905: 'Just to wish you a Happy Easter. I thought you would like this card. I hope you have not one like it. Please give my love to your Mother – I hope she is better – & accept same yourself.'

Alice to her mother, Mrs Oliver, in Alcester, near Shaftesbury, on 17 September 1906: 'Just a card. Hope you are better. I did not go up to Clara's last night. Am going up one afternoon this week. Thank you for letter. It is much colder here in Bournemouth today.'

The children's paddling pool from the Sandhill, in a card posted in 1905

The Chine's successor playground in 2008

You can still just glimpse White Lodge and Chine Hotel in 2008

reinstated and the land train re-routed to run through the chine. Coloured bricks mark the former shape of the pool and stream, which now flows underground, with a children's play area having taken its place.

Stucco-white Victorian boarding houses in Undercliff Road, 2008

E.C. to Miss J. L. Collens in Gloucester House, South Farnborough, Hampshire, on 4 November 1906: **'We walked by here yesterday afternoon. It's lovely. Shall be at Farnborough Station soon after 9 p.m. tomorrow Monday.'**

To Percy Biggs at 55 Springfield Road, Cotham, Bristol, on 5 June 1909:
'I am getting on very well indeed. The weather has changed & things are looking up. I think you will like it here very much. I have been over to Swanage this morn, with Allan & a friend of his. Expecting Claud every minute. Hope you & Father are getting on all right. Fond love. Yours, Mother. (Do not expect me until Monday or Tuesday.)

Madge, staying at 7 Westby Road, Boscombe, to Miss Linda James at 5 Marlow Road, Maidenhead, 9 April 1910: **'This is a glorious place & the weather is beautiful. I will write when I get time. We go out after breakfast, come in for dinner, tea & supper but do not stay in at all. How do you like the book God's Good Man? I have only time to write this, we are going out again now.'**

Agnes to Miss Dora Denman at Firs Home, Trinity Road, Bournemouth, sometime during the reign of George V: **'Dearest Dora, I have just heard I am starting my holiday next week so I shall not be seeing you as usual. I hope you are feeling better... My sister will be calling to see you sometime during next week. It may be after visiting hours but I don't expect Sister would mind do you?'**

May to Miss Nell Pike at 3 High Street, Stour Provost, Dorset, in 1937: **'Have been spending a week here with my cousin. Thanks so much for sending me on Winnie's new name etc. We called at Dalarran coming down here so Lou let me read your letter. Glad everything went off alright.'**

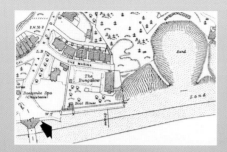

HONEYCOMBE CHINE

The lesser chine at Boscombe, on the eastern side of the approach to the sands, is Honeycombe Chine. Beyond it, Portman Ravine provided a path down to the beach from Wentworth Lodge. This was built in 1873 by the 1st Viscount Portman of Bryanston House, near Blandford. Wentworth Lodge was the wealthy family's seaside villa. The estate was sold for housing development in 1922. Wentworth Lodge was incorporated into Wentworth Milton Mount School for girls – later known as Wentworth College – which resisted co-education until shortly before closure in 2008.

Major developments were taking place in 2008. Offshore, sand from Portman Ravine was being lowered in bags, 225 metres offshore, to create a hectare-sized reef for the benefit of surfers. The idea is to put a spin and swirl into the waves by creating a series of underwater obstructions. Mark Smith, the town's director of tourism, explained that the £3 million project in groyne compartments 23 to 26 has been funded by the sale of an 'under-used' car-park to Barratt Homes. A further £5 million is being spent on refurbishing Boscombe Spa and 'revitalising' its Overstrand complex.

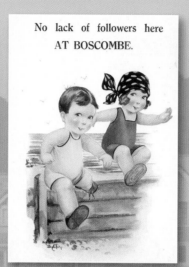

No lack of followers here AT BOSCOMBE.

After the groynes, in a happy card from the 1930s

Boscombe beach and Overstrand in 1908

Boscombe beach and Overstrand in 1910

To Miss Lilly Bradley, Gladstone House, Hartington Road, 'Southend-on-Sea, on 18 July 1906: **'We are sitting down on Boscombe sands. We have been down all the morning & we are not going to get home until 4 o'clock. We have had some cakes & lemonade. We can get any thing at the little shop.'**

Laura Montsourey to Miss Irene Legh-Powell, Fernleigh, Hurstmonceux, Sussex, on 22 July 1912: **'I am venturing to send you my thanks for your kind congratulations for my engagement. I hope you did not lose all your luggage; otherwise you might be arrested in your own country as a spy. Please give my kind regards to [list]. When are you going to write to me?'**

Elsie to Mr Walter Sherwood, 5 Egerton Mansions, Brompton Road, London SW, on 9 June 1922: **'I wish you Many Happy Returns of your past birthday. Better late than never.'**

Onshore, below Ocean Heights, the multi-storey Honeycombe Beach apartments are also taking shape.

Honeycombe beach in 2008

Sand for the surfers' reef beside the Honeycombe Beach development, 2008

The newly-cut zig-zag on a card posted in 1908

X/ This is where the murder took place on the cliffs.

Postcard with murder spot annotation, December 1921

FISHERMAN'S WALK BEACH

Bournemouth's third seaside district was first called Southbourne-on-Sea by Dr Thomas Armetriding Compton (1838-1925). Practising in Bournemouth from 1866, he bought 230 acres – including a mile of cliffs – from General Frederick Cleveland, in 1870. The land contained pastures, two woods, three cottages and a Coastguard Station. The first new house was built by Henry Reeve (1813-95) of *The Times* and the *Edinburgh Review*, beside Foxholes, a wild wood on the north-east side of Stourcliff, in 1874. When he took up residence, in April 1876, he achieved an ambition which he had confided to his diary four years earlier:

> '**I have taken a great fancy to the spot and should be very well contented to end my days there, gazing on that magnificent view of the coast and sea.'**

Dr Compton added Cellarsfield Farm, including the wood at Foxholes, to his property portfolio in 1875. For a time, however, these coastal holdings and General Cleveland's residual Stourwood Estate were a barrier to development and Pokesdown was the name that took precedence all the way to the sea. Foxholes House became St Cuthbert's School. Stourwood House still stands in Stourwood Road. The only access to the sea used to be via a wooden staircase known as Pokesdown Steps which had cost £55 to construct, in 1890, with Viscount Portman contributing £25.

This was eventually replaced by the present incline pathway. The primacy of Pokesdown seemed assured when, with a population of 4,000, it was established as Pokesdown Urban District under the Local Government Act, 1894. This barely saw out the century, being amalgamated with Bournemouth, in October 1901.

Built in about 1766 by Edmund Bott (1740-80), Stourfield House had been owned by Admiral William Popham, the son of signals pioneer Sir Home Riggs Popham, since 1844. By 1865 the estate included a post office, general stores, bakery, two public houses, two smithies and St James's Church. Then in 1893 the land was sold by the Popham family, and Southbourne was about to burst into life, around the new Grand Avenue and across this entire area between Fisherman's Walk and Clifton Road. Nine hundred plots were staked out between Southbourne Road and Cranleigh Road.

Stourfield House, enlarged into a sanatorium, became a convalescent home for wounded servicemen during the Great War. It was acquired by the British Legion in 1923 and named Douglas House. In 1948 it was taken over by the National Health Service until closure in 1989 which was followed by demolition.

My father's postcard of this spot has an 'X' added to it, with the annotation:

'This is where the murder took place on the cliffs.'

Seafront Office and promenade, 2008

The victim was Miss Irene Wilkins, a cook, whose body was dumped here on 22 December 1921. Thomas Henry Allaway of Windsor Road, a chauffeur, was convicted of the killing and sentenced to death, at Winchester on 7 July 1922.

The distinctive beach kiosk, with its twelve-sized copper canopy, was dismantled in June 1940 when the Royal Engineers fortified Bournemouth beach against the threat of German invasion.

The zig-zag from the sands, 2008

SOUTHBOURNE PIER

Southbourne had its own pier. The Board of Trade authorised its construction at a point 4,000 yards east of the stream emerging from Boscombe Chine. Designed by Archibald Smith, it was built in 1887-88, and extended seawards for 300 feet. Iron girders rested 'upon iron piles, screwed by machinery into a solid foundation below the sand'.

On the opening day, 2 August 1888, more than 1,200 people filed through the turnstiles, according to the pier-master, Captain Legg. Paddle-steamers were scheduled to call but often failed to return – complaining of adverse conditions – if there was a change of currents or wind.

The pier's promoters, Cox & Bazalgette, also built Bournemouth's first promenade as an Undercliff Esplanade. Costing £12,000, it was 100 feet in width, with *Bright's Guide to Bournemouth* proclaiming its strength in 1898:

> 'It consists of a solid concrete wall, rising about nine feet above the beach level, with foundations extending some nine or ten feet below it, and placed on a bed of hard sand or solid clay. The wall is of enormous strength, being built as a practical monolith of the very best cement concrete... A handsome stone terrace of dwelling houses has been erected upon the Undercliff.'

The Wrecked Pier, Southbourne

Wrecked pier and promenade on a card posted in 1906

Broken sea well, after removal of pier debris, from what is now Warren Edge Close in 1912

All were soon to be in peril. Rough seas became the norm and the pier's downfall was caused by double gales on 28 December 1900 and 3 January 1901. Pier, promenade and houses were wrecked. Their derelict remains were not cleared away until 1907.

Featureless is now the word, for 2008

Southbourne beach is the right-hand blob on the map

HENGISTBURY HEAD

Detached from Southbourne by flat ground where the River Stour ran to the sea until shortly before the end of the last Ice Age, the last bastion of Bournemouth's gravel plateau rises to 119 feet at Warren Hill. From the extremity of Hengistbury Head, a long groyne points towards the Beerpan Rocks, a quarter of a mile offshore. These mark the pre-Victorian coastline.

Its attrition rate was accelerated by quarrying for ironstone boulders. A great gash in the hilltop, now landscaped with a little lake, is angled towards an opening in the marshes beside the Mudeford spit, where Holloway's Quay was where the 'doggers' were loaded on to barges.

Long before that, this was a busy place, being the main Iron Age port for the Durotrigic peoples who built the Wessex hill-forts and traded with their kinsmen on the other side of the Channel. Their wharves, huts, and the promontory itself were protected by the palisaded Double Dykes earthworks which still cut off the peninsula. Coin hoards and quern-stones were among the finds during excavations before the Great War when a short-lived golf course was being built across the main settlement.

Earlier prehistoric settlement evidence dates back to the Bronze Age, including several Bronze burial mounds, but began in the Mesolithic period – at around 6000 BC – with scooped-out shelters surrounded by middens and a scattering of worked flints of finger-size or smaller. All this seems abandoned and wild but only a timely recession saved it from becoming the English Xanadu.

Millionaire London department store owner Gordon Selfridge commissioned architect Philip Tilden to designed the biggest house in Europe. It was to have comprised two palatial castles,

Hugh to Mr J. H. Hoppe in Piddington, near Bicester, Oxfordshire, in 1936: **'How's yourself? Icy cold here. Rain & hail. Love from us all.'**

Uncle H and Aunty M to Mr and Mrs N. Lawrence at 605 Tonbridge Road, Maidstone, Kent on 4 July 1954: **'We are having a nice time, although the weather isn't too good. I expect you know this spot. We went here Wednesday. Hope both well.'**

HENGISTBURY HEAD

Hengistbury Head from inside the Double Dykes, in a view posted in 1954

Hengistbury Head from Southbourne beach, 2002

astride the 119-feet high summit of the headland, inside complex outworks amounting to four miles of towers, turrets and walls. The dream died with the Wall Street Crash and Selfridge sold the land to Bournemouth Corporation for £25,250 on 6 May 1930.

The promontory beyond the Double Dykes earthworks was inside the boundary of the borough of Christchurch. These 357 acres were transferred to the county borough of Bournemouth on 1 April 1932 (bringing the town's area to its current extent of 11,627 acres).

Making a splash closer to the headland, 1997

From Southbourne beach in 2008

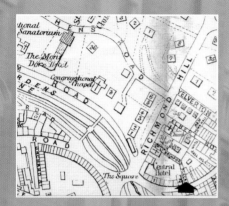

TAPPS ARMS INN

The Tapps Arms Inn, in a cul-de-sac facing North Road (now widened into Old Christchurch Road) on its northern side, was the earliest surviving building in the town centre until demolition in 1885. It was built 1809 and stood 200 yards east-north-east from the rustic bridge over the Bourne Stream. The next public house at that time was the New Inn at Iford.

Bournemouth's wayside hostelry was named for the lord of the manor, Sir George Tapps, who had in 1805 obtained an Inclosure Commissioner's Award over the liberty of Westover, with other big landowner William Dean. Lewis Tregonwell bought the inn and modestly re-named it the Tregonwell Arms. The licensee in 1831 was George Barrow who was followed in 1837 by George Fox.

Fox then became Bournemouth's first postmaster, having obtained a franchise from the Post Office to act as a receiving officer for mail, in 1839. That was immediately before the Royal Mail embraced the world's first pre-paid stamps with the advent of the 'Penny Black' in 1840.

George Fox remained a publican until 1848 when he moved to nearby Beckford House – also on the north side of North Road – midway downhill towards the Square. There he continued as postmaster, until 1861, and also traded as a bookseller and stationer, as well as part-time taxidermist. Honeysuckle and ivy, planted by Mr Atwell, shrouded the porch. Like colonial houses in New England, the building took on an almost iconic status, far beyond its years.

Tastes were changing, however, and on 31 December 1883 the Tregonwell Arms relinquished its licence. The Countess of Cottenham re-opened it on 16 February 1884 as the Blue Ribbon Coffee Tavern. Teetotaller zealots proved disastrous for business. Closure followed and the

The Tapps Arms in its Tregonwell Arms guise, circa 1882

building was demolished in February 1885. It was the year in which the population of Bournemouth topped 25,000.

Beckford Road (now Post Office Road) was cut through 38 feet of the west side of the site, leaving a plot 25 feet wide and 75 feet deep on what is now the corner of Post Office Road and the pedestrianised section Old Christchurch Road. The town's first purpose-built Post Office was built further along the new road and postal operations for the growing town moved there moved from the Quadrant, in Old Christchurch Road, on 1 August 1896.

The corner at 27, 29 & 31 Old Christchurch Road became local head office for the Westminster Bank, until its merger with the National Provincial Bank, and offices for the Woolwich Building Society until its demutualisation. Those rooms are currently empty.

Stamp collectors from around the world made a pilgrimage to Post Office Road during the 46th Philatelic Congress which was held in Bournemouth in May 1964.

Post Office Road and what was the Woolwich

CENTRAL STATION

Here, in 1885, the railway station was built on the eastern side of Holdenhurst Road, before the direct line arrived under the bridge from Brockenhurst, in 1888. The two original platforms beside the main road were 800 feet long and partially covered by a high glass roof. Waiting and refreshment rooms were provided, as well as ground on each side of the tracks for carriages and taxi-cabs. The journey time, from London Waterloo, was cut to three hours.

Beneath the station clock on the up-platform, on the morning of 22 March 1898, ailing ex-Premier William Ewart Gladstone made his last impromptu speech. Having abandoned a winter break in Cannes, to stay at Forest House in Grove Road, he was told by doctors that he was dying. He returned from the Central Station to the land of his forefathers and died at Harwarden Castle on 19 May that year.

The railway through Bournemouth, from Waterloo to Weymouth, was the last main-line to be worked by steam power, until full electrification in July 1967. Outwardly, Bournemouth Central still looks much the same, except that it is now simply Bournemouth Station (after the elimination of Bournemouth West and Boscombe). The up-line approach, however, is very different, having lost the town's Royal Mail sorting office and main depot of Kennedy's builders merchants, but gained Halfords and Staples. On the other side of Holdenhurst Road the South Western Hotel is now Sound Circus night-club.

> Kit to Miss Edith Cosen, 2 Wooperton Terrace, Weymouth, on 12 January 1906:
> 'Just a card to let you know I haven't forgotten you. What do you think of this – nearly as big as Weymouth is . . . hope you are well. I had a letter from N Wednesday; all quite well. Love to yourself and my dear black boy.'

An up train, steaming for London, in a card posted in 1905

Another up train, taking on water, towards the end of mainline steam in the mid-1960s

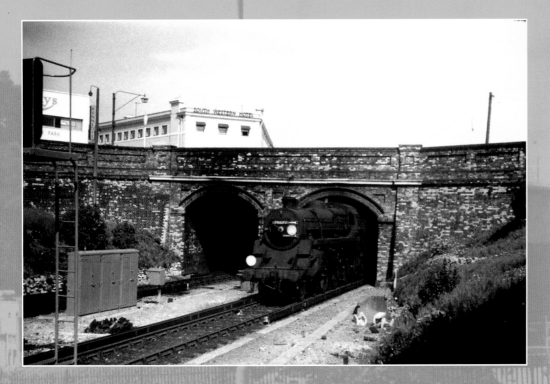

Engine 75077 and a down train from London coming through the bridge under Holdenhurst Road in the mid-1960s

'L' to Mrs K. Shipp, 6 Eden Grove, Wimborne, on 4 August 1904: **'I shall be coming tomorrow by the train that leaves here at 11, arrive at 12.2. Hope you are both well. I feel a little better. Will you ask Fred if he will be so kind as to see if there is a message from his father.'**

L.C, to Mr F. Aburrow, 89 Friar Street, Reading, on 20 February 1906: **'Card [of the Bournemouth Express] to start your collection of railway trains. I wrote this letter last night but didn't have the chance to post it.'**

Glen, staying at 4 West Station Terrace, Queens Road, to Mrs M. Lewis, The Poplars, East Coker, near Yeovil, on 20 August 1917: **'Arrived alright. Lovely weather. The train was plenty full enough and was 30 minutes late. Not so bad for wartime. Managed to leave Vic's parcel. Please send key of bag in sideboard & half pound of sugar.'**

Bournemouth Station can still just be glimpsed from Holdenhurst Road, 2008

South West Trains service for London Waterloo leaving Bournemouth

OMNIBUS and COACH STATION

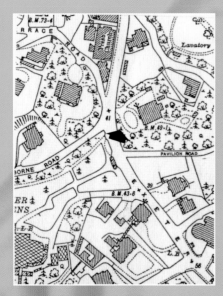

The open-air stopping area beside Exeter Road covered the site of thatched Portman Lodge. This was built in 1811, initially for Captain Lewis Tregonwell's butler, Symes, though after

Tregonwell's death his widow, Mrs Harriet Tregonwell, moved into the lodge and died here on 5 April 1846. Its name was Tregonwell Lodge until it became the home of Edward Berkeley, 1st Viscount Portman. On 3 June 1922, Portman Lodge was gutted by fire. Then rebuilt, though as an ordinary looking house, it was demolished at the end of the decade for the omnibus depot.

The other building that succumbed for the same purpose was Lainston Villa and its Exeter Lane cul-de-sac. This was the residence of Christopher Crabbe Creeke, the town's first surveyor, and the Bournemouth Commissioners met here from 1858 to 1875.

The Hants & Dorset Motor Services depot opened on 9 March 1931 and co-hosted long-distance Royal Blue Coaches though their garages were in Green Road at Charminster. They have now moved on and the land is back in limbo, doing service for National Car Parks, with the precise sites of Portman Lodge and Lainston Villa currently growing weeds.

Portman Lodge and St Andrew's Church in a card posted in 1910

The site became the Omnibus & Coach Station in 1931

Weeds, cars, litter and St Andrew's Church (sans spire) in 2008

The Square from the junction of Gervis Place and Old Christchurch Road, 1865

THE SQUARE (Looking West)

Decoy House and its wildfowling pond lay on the upstream side of a rustic bridge. That was replaced by a brick structure, in 1849, funded jointly by the Gervis Estate and well-heeled residents. A thatched cottage here was the holiday home of Maria Amelia de Bourbon (1782-1866), the last Queen of France, after her exile in 1848. Her neighbours in summer-time were the Duke of Argyll and the Duke and Duchess of Montrose.

Two semi-detached cottages stood on the south side of the Square where Bobby's drapery store was built. In 1899 the stream was put into a culvert and the six-way cross-roads replaced by a small round island with tall wrought iron lamp standards in the middle.

Bournemouth's tramway system began from Pokesdown to the Lansdowne in July 1902 and was extended westwards, via the Square, to Westbourne, December 1902. The line up Richmond

Bournemouth Centenary Fetes, The Square.

No. 5.

The Square decked out with bunting for Bournemouth's centenary celebrations in July 1910

To Miss Mab Hitchcock, Throop House, Throop, on 14 December 1906: 'Hope you did not want me to come down to . . . It is so rough and I cannot get away very well. Expect you are going to Bourne this afternoon. I have just wrote [sic] to Mr H: come back from London. Yet I expect he has enjoyed himself. Hope you got back safe the other night. Will come down Sunday in the morning. Love to all. Ta Ta.'

Will to Mrs Radford, Kelvin Grove, St Sampsons, Guernsey, on 29 July 1909: 'Dear Mother, This is a P.C. of the Square, Bournemouth. We will arrive in Guernsey Sunday morning. Have no time to write more as I have to catch train to Southampton.'

A.K. Cooper to Mrs W.F. Mumford & friends, 2 Medina Terrace, Cowes, Isle of Wight, on 27 March 1910: 'Bournemouth Y.M.C.A. Easter greetings! Came here Thursday; returning Tuesday morning. Have enjoyed splendid weather, particularly today. About 60 young fellows staying here & having a good time. Kind regards to you all & hope Frank is progressing well these fine days.'

Pam to Miss M. Smith, 10 West Bridge, Leicester, on 23 August 1910: 'Received letter alright Tuesday morning. Glad to hear you are all getting on alright. We went over to Swanage on Monday. Very nice trip & everything passed off alright except that Huw was trying to walk on air & came down flopa. Went to Tilly Whim Caves which is a long way & all up hill from the town. Went also into the Light-house which is kept very nice and clean. The Keeper explained all the doings to us.'

Hill was added in 1903. A side loop was laid around the south side of the square, between the outer line and its circle of grass, in 1906. The layout at the Square then remained unchanged until 1921 when the central building did at last go square. Meanwhile, by 1908, the tram network had been extended in both directions, to Tuckton and Christchurch in the east, and Parkstone and Poole in the west.

The motive power was from conduits until May 1911 when the system switched to overhead cables. Though the Square was the central terminus, through-working there was not achieved until 27 February 1921.

The round island was redesigned as a square in 1925 with a shelter being built around a clock-tower provided by Captain Harry B. Norton. The last Bournemouth tram ran in 1936 with No. 85 being saved from the breakers and preserved at Mallard Road Depot. The Square was the hub of trolley bus network from 1933 until 1969. By that time it was a busy roundabout, with the clock standing alone in dense vegetation, and subways were put under it in 1975. Pedestrianisation followed in the 1980s.

Tram from the same angle, over towards Bernard Knight 's store in Commercial Road, with the conductor being the author's 14-year-old father, Ted Legg, in 1916

Towards Commercial Road with the Square as a roundabout in the 1960s

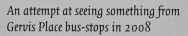

An attempt at seeing something from Gervis Place bus-stops in 2008

Oswald to Miss Tummer, Ravensbury, Upwey, near Weymouth, on 20 May 1911: **'Very glad to learn Father** [Revd. James Tummer] **is so much more lively. Very cold & miserable to-day. We must try & manage a day some time later on together.'**

W.D. to Miss Ida A. White, 5 Monmouth Road, North End, Portsmouth, on 11 July 1927: **'Yesterday heard the great Bournemouth preacher Dr Jones and enjoyed the sermon very much. A wonderful preacher. His sermons have been on the wireless. Thunderstorm in the evening. I do hope the next will do you good. Will write again on my return. The Needles can just be seen in the distance. Expect to get home Wednesday evening.'**

H.C.K. to Mrs Pavy in Cheshire, on 22 February 1910: **'Been here since Saturday. Weather very bad but improving a little today. Back on Saturday I think. Hope you are all well.'**

From further around the bend, from the entrance to the Gardens, in 2008

THE SQUARE (Looking East)

The north side of Old Christchurch Road, on its corner with Richmond Hill, has been dominated since 1855-58 by the five-storey Hotel Empress. Its ground floor became the National Provincial Bank, which is now the National Westminster, since its merger with the Westminster Bank. Beside it were the six shops of Southbourne Terrace, with apartments above, which were built in 1863 by Henry Joy who in 1868 grubbed out the rustic bridge over the Bourne Stream and replaced it with a standard brick one.

Above the Empress Hotel, up Richmond Hill, were the Central Hotel and Punshon Memorial Wesleyan Church, until these were demolished by German bombs in a lunchtime air-raid on Sunday 23 May 1943. Bristol & West House took their place in the late 1950s.

The Square, towards Richmond Chambers, the Central Hotel, Empress Hotel and Gervis Place in 1906

The lasting name in Southbourne Terrace, at Nos. 11 and 13 Old Christchurch Road, has been that of booksellers W. H. Smith & Son. This used to have the best tea-rooms in Bournemouth, on the first floor, with Bacon & Bricknell being its three-piece band. They continued to play until 1957.

Richard Tyrrell's drapery shop on the south side of Old Christchurch Road, known as Commercial House, was sold to Plummer Roddis Ltd in 1891. Their competitors next door were

Bright and Son, later Bright & Coulson Ltd, which was founded by retired missionary Frederick J. Bright. It became Dingles. Well-known names on the south side, dating from 1915, included drapers Bobby & Co. (which became Debenhams) and Woolworths – destroyed by a wartime bomb – which was replaced by Boots the Chemist.

The Bournemouth Graphic commented on the laying of tram lines up Richmond Hill in 1903: **'This gradient has been a very expensive luxury and is possibly one which will result in a loss of profits for some years to come.'**

(Top left) After the blizzard on 25 April 1908

(Top right) Taxi rank, tram-lines and the hotels on a sunny day in 1908

Horse-drawn cab and motorised taxi, plus tram, with greetings for 1912

Royal Blue charabanc beside Richmond
Chambers, 30 July 1914

Obscura centre-piece and a gondola over the
Gardens in July 2008

Closer view of the Obscura and former Empress Hotel, in 2008

The Square as a square, around Harry Norton's clock-tower, about 1928

EXETER ROAD

Heading south from what became the Square, this was Decoy Pond Road when Captain Lewis Dymoke Tregonwell lunched with his wife Harriet at the nearby Tapps Arms on 14 July 1810. He had patrolled the coast with the Dorset Volunteer Rangers – the Dorset Yeomanry – through the Napoleonic invasion threat at the turn of the century. Harriet (formal name Henrietta) persuaded Lewis to buy land from lord of the manor Sir George Tapps to build a seaside residence. A plot of 8.5 acres on the east side of 'Public Road No. 7', between Decoy House and the Bourne Mouth, was acquired for £179-11s-0d.

On this the Tregonwells built a villa which was originally known as The Mansion (later Exeter House, now incorporated into Exeter Hotel) and a lodge for their butler, Symes. This was Tregonwell Lodge, later Portman Lodge, when it was the home of Viscount Portman. Harriet's father was Henry William Portman, of Orchard Portman in Somerset, and Bryanston in Dorset.

The Tregonwells' main homes were Cranborne Lodge, in Cranborne, and Anderson Manor, near Bere Regis. The building at Bournemouth took place in 1811 and their first seaside holiday there was the following spring, from April 1812. For the Tregonwells this was a retreat rather than a residence. By 1820 it was being let to the Marchioness of Exeter whose name became permanently attached both to the house and the road.

The distinctive building since 1888 has been St Andrew's Church – the town's 'Scotch church' as it was known – which migrated from the corner of the Square that became the Empress Hotel. The size was substantial, with a nave 88 feet long by 54 feet wide, to be precise. It has since gone the way of mammon and lost its spire in the process.

That was a real loss to the skyline, as *Bright's Guide to Bournemouth* confirms: **'It rises to a height of 170 feet, calculated from the pavement to the top of the weathercock, which is fixed in a vane.'**

Horse-bus before the trams in a view from the Square to St Andrew's Church, in 1899

Yellow cabs and red and yellow buses, to a spire-less St Andrew's, in 2008

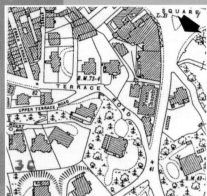

Raphael Tuck card caption: '**St Andrew's Presbyterian Church is in Exeter Road, Bournemouth. It is a handsome edifice, seating 700 persons. Its tower and spire are built of terra-cotta and tiles. The rose window at its north end is much admired. The church was opened in 1888.**'

Shop-fronts from Debenhams and the Moon in the Square, in J. D. Wetherspoon House, to Rebbeck estate agents in 2008

The iconic home of municipal music in the British Isles, 1902

Similar view, hand-coloured, posted in 1905

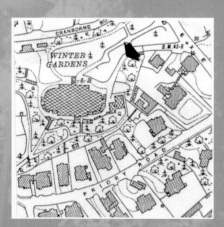

WINTER GARDENS

Having been originally laid out by the Tregonwell family as their Cranborne Gardens, in 1860 the pleasure ground on the south-west side of Exeter Road was redesigned by the next owner, Robert Kerley, for the new craze of archery. It opened to the public in August 1862. Marquees for parties were a frequent sight, such as that for HRH the Nawab Nazim of Bengal, on 24 September 1870. In 1872, Kerley died, and a Bournemouth Winter Garden Company was formed in 1873 to build a fashionable glass pavilion there for holding social events in a miniature jungle of exotic plants.

In 1875 a price was agreed with London contractors Fletcher, Lowdnes & Co. for the building of a great conservatory, at a cost of £12,000. There was also to be a skating rink in the grounds.

The latter opened first, on 15 January 1876, and the Winter Gardens followed on 16 January 1877, with the honours being conducted by Sir Henry Drummond Wolff MP. Commercially, the project proved a failure, so in 1893 the Corporation of Bournemouth leased the Winter Gardens for adaptation into a concert hall, to provide a home for Dan Godfrey's military-style band which had become the Bournemouth Municipal Orchestra. Bournemouth Corporation bought the building, from Hector Monro, in 1908 but did not acquire the ground on which it stood until 1929.

Meanwhile. the 'Conservatory' or 'Glasshouse' as the 'little Crystal Palace' was also known, hosted concerts conducted by the greatest British composers of the age – in order of appearance Manns, Stanford, Parry, Mackenzie, Holst, Harty, Elgar, Coates, Vaughan Williams and Bliss. Sibelius came to conduct Finlandia in 1921. Dame Ethel Smyth, a brick-throwing suffragette composer, worked on Lloyd George to get Godfrey a knighthood.

The diamond jubilee of the Winter Gardens was marked by Sir Dan Godfrey's farewell concert on 16 November 1935 and the final event, which closed a week later, was a pageant of Wessex history. Then the old Winter Gardens was dismantled and the musicians moved to the Pavilion.

Illuminated to moonlight with candles in coloured jars, in about 1930

The Winter Gardens was replaced by a £30,000 Indoor Bowling Green, claimed as 'undoubtedly the finest in the world' with eight 120 feet rinks of green Rolphelt carpet, 'one of which is reserved for the use of ladies'.

After the war, the Bournemouth Municipal Orchestra gave its first concert in a rebuilt Winter Gardens on 18 October 1947, with a performance conducted by Rudolf Schwarz. The Western Orchestra Society Ltd took over management of the musicians under Charles Groves, as the reformed Bournemouth Symphony Orchestra, and their first concert in the new Winter Gardens took place on 7 October 1954. Guest conductor was Sir Thomas Beecham. Here wartime fighter pilot Terry Spencer caught up with the Beatles and photographed them on their first national tour.

A 1923-dated memorial tablet to composer Sir Hubert Parry, who gave us the famous tune 'Jerusalem' to words by William Blake, was put into store in the Central Library at the Lansdowne, and re-erected in the second Winter Gardens in 1964:

> **'Born in this town February 27, 1848. A great musician whose influence on British music will always be remembered.'**

The plaque is presumably once again in limbo as the site is now the Winter Gardens Car Park. The last concert here by Bournemouth Symphony Orchestra took place on 20 January 2002, after which it decamped to Poole Arts Centre.

To Miss Crump, 2 Station Parade, Balham, London SW, on 17 April 1905: **'What a lucky holiday we are having! We found a mackintosh in your bed-room and shall bring it home with us. We had another glorious morning and spent it at Branksome Chine – but while at dinner it has come over very cloudy. Hope to reach Waterloo at 4.10 on Thursday.'**

Daisy to Miss Lizzie Edwards, Roborough, Cavendish Place, Bournemouth, on 13 November 1906: **'Thank you very much for P.C. Eliza & I hope to come to Bournemouth on Tuesday, and will come and see you. I hope you will soon feel stronger.'**

'M' to Mrs Vacher, Mount Cottage, Whitchurch, Hampshire, on 20 August 1906: **'Dear Mother, We are going to Salisbury tomorrow morning and shall come down by the 10 o'clock train at night. It has been very hot here today. Went to see Uncle Joe & family Tuesday morning.'**

Sir Hugh Allen, quoted in *The Times*, in the 1930s: **'Bournemouth is a striking example of what municipalities could do for music, and it leads the world in that respect.'**

(Bottom left) That spot is still leafy but with nothing behind it in 2008

(Bottom right) 'Welcome to Winter Gardens Car Park' in 2008

BEALES

When he began trading as 'The Oriental Fancy Fair House' in newly-built No. 3 St Peter's Terrace, just in time for Christmas in 1881, 33-year-old John Elmes Beale from Weymouth began a Bournemouth dynasty. By 1905 he owned and occupied all four shops and apartments in the three-storey building and the stage was set for its replacement by a multi-storey department store.

Built by W. A. Hoare, in 1906, this became the provincial equivalent of Gordon Selfridge's superstore in London's Oxford Street. A seventh storey and a clock were added in 1929.

The store came to a dramatic end, from bombs and then fire, in a lunchtime attack by German Focke Wulf FW 190 bombers on 23 May 1943. The building was empty, however, as it happened to be a Sunday. The clock collapsed later into the street when a rescue worker was killed by falling masonry.

Through the remaining years of war and those of austerity the store operated from cabins beside blitzed cellars. A seven-storey replacement arose on the site in the 1950s.

The second Beales fire took place on the afternoon of Monday 7 November 1966. Somehow a rocket was ignited as unsold Bonfire Night fireworks were being packed for return to manufacturers. A shop worker with an extinguisher failed to control the incident. Fireworks exploded and flashed across the toy department on the first floor. Store boss Anthony Beale, on the second floor, gave the order for evacuation as smoke rose through the building.

(Bottom left) Beales in 1929, before the addition of an extra storey and clock

(Bottom right) Beales bombed, with the iconic clock resting in Old Christchurch Road, 23 May 1943

Workers mustered in the safety of St Peter's churchyard, with the roll call accounting for all but one of the 600 staff, as firemen rescued the missing person. Mrs M. E. Mears, an elderly seamstress, won a round of applause as firemen whisked her from the sixth-floor veranda, on to a turntable ladder. Another 30 people were retrieved from windows. Fifteen customers and staff were taken to hospital with burns, cuts and shock. By this time the fire had been doused.

Beales as rebuilt, photographed on the centenary of the original Fancy Fair, in 1981

Beales from Old Christchurch Road, after partial pedestrianisation, in 2008

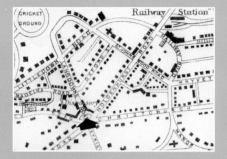

THE LANSDOWNE

The Lansdowne is the alternative town centre with multiple junctions similar to those at the Square. The name came from Lansdowne Villas, dating from 1863, which comprised one detached house and a pair of semi-detached dwellings beside Christchurch Road, on the east side of the junction with Holdenhurst Road. Lansdowne House was built on this corner in 1868.

There was also a Lansdowne Crescent which strengthened the Somerset associations. Lansdowne Hill in Bath provided the title for William Petty, 1st Marquis of Lansdowne (1737-1805), though he was generally known as Lord Shelburne. There is a Dorset link, with Abbotsbury and Melbury, as Henry Petty-Fitzmaurice, 3rd Marquis of Lansdowne (1780-1863) married Lady Louisa Emma Fox-Strangways, the fifth daughter of Henry Thomas, 2nd Earl of Ilchester, in 1808.

Lansdowne House was pulled down in 1890 and work began in 1891 on what was initially called the Palace Hotel. Architecturally flamboyant, its name triggered a tradename dispute, which threatened to end in litigation. So it was as the Hotel Metropole that it opened in 1893. Advertisements promised modernity:

'Due South. Near Golf Links. Magnificent Ball-Room. Electric Light throughout. Passenger Lift to each floor. Buses meet all Trains.'

'F' to Mrs T. Lacy in Borden, near Sittingbourne, Kent, on 11 September 1905: 'Basket arrived safely this evening. Have not unpacked it. Many thanks for it & for letter this morning. Will write perhaps tomorrow or Wednesday.'

J. & W. Lane to Miss Gladys Mason, 26 Villiers Road, Cricklewood, on 14 September 1909: 'We are spending part of our holiday here . . . This is a lovely place. Have been to Swanage, Weymouth, and Ventnor, Isle of Wight by boat. Enjoyed trips very much.'

55 BOURNEMOUTH — Hotel Metropole. — LL

The splendour of the Hotel Metropole in 1913

Bright's Guide to Bournemouth endorsed the claims: 'The **interior of the Hotel is a marvel of modern luxury and art; there are some 200 rooms; elegant private suites, all facing south; Ladies' Coffee and Morning Rooms; the Drawing Room deserves special mention; it is considered one of the finest in the kingdom, and is furnished with exquisite taste. The cuisine is all that can be desired; the "Musical Dinner" is served at separate tables at 7 p.m. A ball is held in the grand Salon every Saturday evening.'**

Many died when the hotel was ripped apart by a German bomb in 1943.

The Hotel Metropole was destroyed by a German bomb at lunchtime on Sunday 23 May 1943. This was the most calamitous of the explosions that day. Seventy-seven civilians were killed across the town but no publicity was given to military casualties, with the bodies of at least 24 servicemen being removed from the Hotel Metropole. Most were air crew from Canada and Australia. Several hotels and schools had been requisitioned for Dominion airmen who were inspected in the Pavilion by King George VI and Queen Elizabeth on 23 October 1941.

The Metropole name survives with the Metropole Bar in Holdenhurst Road but the main part of the building remained a bomb site until the late 1950s. Redeveloped as the ten-storey Royal London House, it is now owned by Bournemouth University.

(Bottom left) The bomb site is now the Metropole Bar (beside the bus) and Royal London House, 2008

(Bottom right) From the other side of the roundabout, currently plastic-covered, in 2008

Emmie to Mrs Gertie Goodland, 20 Trinity Terrace, Weymouth, on 12 July 1932: 'All being well if fine shall be at Weymouth tomorrow (Wed). I will call & see you all, coming by the 9.42 arrive 11.12. Trusting you are all well.'

Lizzie to Mrs Rapson, 5 High Street, Ilchester, Somerset, on 25 October 1932: 'Dear Sister, Just a line to let you know that we are alright but the weather is so bad we can't go anywhere we want in Bournemouth, Friday, and it poured with rain all the time. We should like to go in once more, so are going to try it Tuesday if it keep fine & shall be coming home Friday.'

Kathleen Gorringe to Miss W. Neighbour, Crofton, 198 Capstone Road, Bournemouth, on 31 December 1947: 'Thank you so much for your most useful Xmas gift. I hope to record many happy days in 1948. My best wishes to you both for 1948. Hope the stamps I brought along have all been sold.'

LOWER GARDENS

Sir George Gervis MP (1795-1842) began his Marine Village in 1836 but died so young that his heir was a minor, and Westover Villas – along Westover Road from the Bath Hotel to Gervis Place – were the only part of the vision that was completed in his lifetime. They were designed by Christchurch architect Benjamin Ferrey. He was succeeded by Decimus Burton who had designed the Triumphal Arch at Hyde Park Corner in 1828.

Burton began in 1848 to turn paddocks and the Bourne Meadows into Westover Pleasure Gardens. The Bournemouth Commissioners took over the project and by the spring of 1873 these had become the Lower Pleasure Gardens. Upstream, on the other side of the Square, George Durrant had bought further lengths of Bourne Stream meadows from the Branksome Estate, in 1851. Durrant parted with the land to the Bournemouth Commissioners in 1873 in order to create the Upper Pleasure Gardens over the next decade.

Confusingly, both the Lower Gardens and Upper Gardens sometimes appear on maps as the 'Central Gardens' and the Ordnance Survey overcomes the problem by designating them the Lower Central Gardens and Upper Central Gardens.

Victorian-style mosaiculture – carpet bedding design – is still practised. Traditionally, the town crest and Latin 'Pulchritudo et salubritas' (Beauty and health) motto have been depicted with *Alternanthera* for bronze, green, yellow and red, *Echeveria* for grey, *Sedum* for silver and purple, *Klinea* which is greyish-blue, and *Pyrethrum* in its 'Golden Moss' form. The essential attribute for all these plants is that they are both miniature and can be clipped.

The Gardens Bournemouth.

(Top left) Plus grass and flowers in a view posted in 1912

(Top right)
Much the same, plus the opportunity of rising under a helium balloon, in 2008

Closer glimpse across the grass which is shared by pairs of doves and humans, 2008

85

CHILDREN'S CORNER

Fashions change and water now comes with health and safety warnings. This spot is now for nostalgia rather than fun. It extends from a bridge below Pine Walk, downstream, to the rock garden beside the Pavilion.

The Legg family can only recall hordes of paddling youngsters in this busiest section of the Lower Gardens when we were here below the bandstand in the 1950s. The objective was to play with my brother Barrie's yacht though the depth of the keel and flow of the water were hardly conducive to good sailing. We did better with a wooden aircraft carrier, HMS *Ark Royal*, which father had carved during the war. It had the advantage of a flat bottom and was weighted under the hull with a strip of lead. Being sailless it also needed the current.

Bright's Guide to Bournemouth in 1902 described it as:

> **'The Children's Canal which stretches along under the Invalids' Walk. The banks and bed of the portion of stream have here been formed in concrete, and excepting after heavy storms, never contain a depth of more than about six or eight inches of water, so as to be perfectly safe for children, with whom this is a very favourite spot for sailing their miniature yachts.'**

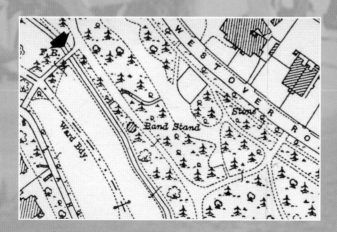

Hordes of kids and the new Pavilion, from the bridge, in 1936

Child-free zone, from the bridge to the Pavilion, in July 2008

Early colour film, in a shot by Edwin Dodshon, downstream to the Pavilion in 1938

Upstream, towards Plummer Roddis Ltd, the drapers in Gervis Place, in 1922

Auntie to Master Jack Cottle in Manners Road, Southsea, on 13 February 1905: '**I am too late to get you a Valentine so I send you a P.C. Hope your lips is getting well. Sorry you lost your teeth, you will look a funny boy. Granny, Grampa & my love to Mama & Daddy. Lots of kisses for you.**'

Ava to Mrs U. Burt in Clarendon Place, Romsey, on 18 November 1905: '**I am well & hope to send off blouse tomorrow (Monday). It is finished but I have not time to pack it today, Saturday.**'

Embossed seasonal version of a standard postcard, to Miss Gladis Sweeting at Lower Farm, Dowlish Wake, Somerset, on 19 December 1906: '**To wish Dear Glady a merry Xmas & a happy New Year.**'

'Y' to Mrs E. Aburrow at 24 Gower Street, Reading:, on 31 March 1909: '**You did not answer my last letter, had begun to think you had departed this life. Sorry to hear you both have colds but trust they are better. Isn't the weather awful . . . Have you seen Mrs Mills lately. If fine on Thursday we are going for a ride to Christchurch. I hear you have a skating ring in Reading now. Have you been to the theatre lately, I went last week. How is Mr & Mrs Hooper & children getting on? I hope all at home are well, also Ade.**'

Daughter to parents, Mr and Mrs C. Whyte at Norwood, West Promenade, Colwyn Bay, sent 7 October 1911: '**Many happy returns of your wedding day tomorrow. I have no time to write more at present, as Mr & Mrs Martin are with us and Peggy as well. Harold has gone over this evening to see Uncle about Brazil as Gerald wants to go there & his father wants an answer on Monday.**'

'M', undated, to Miss K. Penny at the Stores in Bowerchalke, near Salisbury: '**Sorry you could not get as far but shall hope to see you later. Practise a bit & try to come with Mr V. Hope Mrs V. is having a pleasant time. The boys saw her as she went through Shaftesbury.**'

E.M.S., undated, to Miss Jacques in Bristol: '**If ever you go here, I hope it will be for your honeymoon.**'

INVALIDS' WALK

This was Bournemouth's core purpose, Harry Furniss told readers of the *Good Works* journal, in 1891: 'The place exists chiefly for the invalid.'

Bright's Guide to Bournemouth tells us: 'The famed Invalids' Walk must be specially referred to, offering as it does, at all seasons of the year, a most attractive promenade. It runs through the pine-shaded avenue from the [Gervis] Arcade gate down to the stream; here, in storm or shine, is shelter from wind, or shade from sun, while at foot the dry brown carpet, formed by acicular leaves of the pine, affords protection of the damp.

'Another peculiarity of the leafage is that the sun's rays easily penetrate to the stems and trunks, which are thus warmed, and radiate the heat to the surrounding atmosphere. Without dwelling upon the antiseptic properties of the volatile substances which the pines exhale, enough has been said to show that the Invalids' Walk is not merely a name in which is there is nothing. Here on a summer's day numbers of quiet readers will be found occupying the many seats, intent on the interesting literature of our well-stocked libraries, or listening to the excellent band; and in winter, invalids, who in other towns would fear to leave their rooms, may be found leisurely strolling along the dry carpet, and, while enjoying their open-air exercise, bearing record to the healthy climate of the town.'

Bustle and a Bath-chair in the 1890s

The Pine Walk, Central Gardens, Bournemouth.

The caption to a Raphael Tuck postcard: 'The Invalids' Walk of Bournemouth is justly famous for its beautiful pines, which in at least one part fairly roof the pedestrian. Sheltered there from the sea and comfortably seated, the invalid feels himself a convalescent who will soon be well.'

Lott to Miss A. Mitchell, near Schools, Horsmonden, Kent, on an early Edwardian card: 'I am writing a few lines just to wish you many happy returns of the day. Hope you are enjoying your holiday. Love from all.'

J.W.S. to Miss Codling, 86 Rushmore Road, Clapton, London SE, on 23 January 1907: 'A very nice day but cold. We shall be here until Friday. Glad to hear from you. Returning to Kenilworth Hotel Friday afternoon. Leave for home 11.30 Saturday morning.'

Marie to Mrs Perkins, Mayfield Road, Moseley, Birmingham, on 21 August 1907: 'We have just arrived safely and found our way to the old place where I have stayed before. I hope you will forgive all the trouble I may have caused you, but I am very, very grateful. The town seems very full owing to the Regatta I suppose.'

Mrs Frampton to Miss Ada Orrin, 20 High Street, Wandsworth, London SW, on 26 August 1910: 'I hope you had a nice holiday & are feeling better for it. How is that poor ear of yours, better I hope. We are having a nice holiday down here.'

The Pine Walk conversion in 1910

89

It was not until after the Great War that the dubious Invalids' Walk epithet was officially abandoned in favour of the neutral Pine Walk. There is also an aviary, café, bandstand and open-air art displays. These days mobility scooters have made it accessible to the disabled but bicycles remain the ubiquitous vehicle. How times change. In the 1950s we never dared to cycle there.

'M' to Mrs Garrison, 52 Edwards Road, Erdington, Birmingham, on 1 August 1911: **'Sun still shining & all well. Sent you a card from Cherbourg yesterday but do not think you will get it, as I put an English stamp on.'**

To Miss L. Eldridge, Little Forest House, Cliff Road, Bournemouth, on 30 January 1913: **'Very sorry your time to-day will not suit us. We are having tea at 5 p.m. at Wingfield Lodge & have promised to be up in Gladstone Road 6 p.m. as we have promised to spend the evening with some friends. We go back Monday so I am afraid we shall not be able to see you this time. So sorry.'**

Mother to daughter, Miss Sarah Spalding in Burton-on-Trent, 19 February 1902: **'We shall have lunch coming down but shall be very glad of a cup of tea when we arrive home.'**

Eliza to Miss Grace Cockram, 12 Victoria Villas, Lower Mortlake Road, Richmond, on 14 January 1908: **'What cold weather we are having. I don't suppose you can hardly keep yourself warm, I can't. Thank you very much for the present. Give my love to your mother.'**

B.J. to Miss May Aplin, 29 Stephen Street, Taunton, on 25 August 1908: **'Just a card to let you know I'm still alive. I hope you are all very well. Tell your Ma I will write her a long letter soon. I am looking forward to seeing you soon.'**

A similar view posted in 1915

Pine Walk, Bournemouth

Same view, towards the bandstand, in 2008

'B' to Mr J. G. Worsfold, Vima, Long Lane, Church End, Finchley, London N on 31 August 1912: **'Arrived Bournemouth Thursday morning. Good weather so far. On Emperor of India approaching Weymouth. Expecting to have a look over the Dreadnought.'**

Emma to Miss E. A. Hill, Bardon, Wingfield Road, Trowbridge, on 12 May 1913: **'I did wish you could have been here on Saturday & Sunday – the weather was absolutely perfect. Today we have been almost drowned, but now the Sun is beaming on us again.'**

F.E.H. to Mr E. Whalley in Manchester, on 30 August 1930: **'If you come here bring the car as the easiest way of getting about. Well wooded & hilly.'**

F. Deverall to Miss E. Deverall, 41 Western Terrace, Semington Road, Melksham, on 6 August 1935: **'We are having a lovely time here. The weather is ideal. Bournemouth is crowded.'**

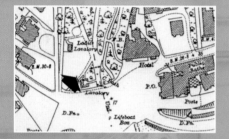

The Pavilion from across the Lower Gardens
in 2008

THE PAVILION

Built on the site of the Belle Vue boarding house which with the Bath Hotel had opened in 1838, the year of Queen Victoria's coronation. Sir Merton Russell-Cotes, followed by Sir Charles Cartwright, championed the cause for building the Pavilion. Costs soared after the Great War and was estimated that £170,000 was needed to develop the Belle Vue site which was not cleared until 1928.

Meanwhile, the foundation stone of the new building had been laid by Alderman Charles Henry Cartwright, on 23 September 1925, with a time-capsule of memorabilia being sealed beneath it in a copper casket. The winning design, in an architectural competition, was that of Londoners G. Wyville Home and Shirley Knight.

The licence from the Belle Vue was transferred to the new Pavilion in February 1929. On 19 March 1929, at noon, HRH the Duke of Gloucester declared it officially open. The general manager was Charles Thomas Hutchison. Mayor Cartwright and Town Clerk Herbert Ashling welcomed their guest. After lunch, Sir Dan Godfrey conducted the Municipal Orchestra, followed by entertainer Stanley Holloway.

It hosted major events, including the Labour Party Conference, such as in 1940 and then with Prime Minister Clement Attlee in 1946, and saw the arrival of Sir Anthony Eden as Premier, for the Conservative Party Conference in 1955.

Outside, down to the Bourne Stream, boulders of Portland and Purbeck stone form one of the largest municipal rock-gardens in the country. Alpine, desert and exotic species from around the world peak in May when *Hypericum olympicium*, *Lithodora diffusa* and *Penstemon pinifolius* are particularly colourful.

The Pavilion from Palace Court Hotel, in a card posted in 1946

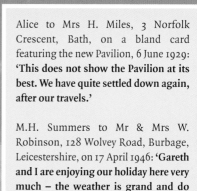

Alice to Mrs H. Miles, 3 Norfolk Crescent, Bath, on a bland card featuring the new Pavilion, 6 June 1929: **'This does not show the Pavilion at its best. We have quite settled down again, after our travels.'**

M.H. Summers to Mr & Mrs W. Robinson, 128 Wolvey Road, Burbage, Leicestershire, on 17 April 1946: **'Gareth and I are enjoying our holiday here very much – the weather is grand and do hope it continues over Easter. We feel heaps better already.'**

'I' to Mrs G. Harris, Longlands, Milton on Stour, Gillingham, Dorset, on 17 August 1960: **'Resting in the sun listening to the band. Wish you were here. We came yesterday [Tuesday] & coming back Friday. See you when we get back.'**

Sea view from above the Lower Gardens, 2008

93

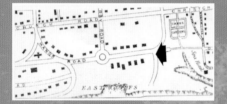

From the same side of Manor Road in 2008

MANOR ROAD

Manor Road has always been an exclusive place to live.

Having spent much of his earlier life on the Riviera, Irish lawyer Hugh McCalmont Cairns, 1st Earl Cairns (1819-85), adopted Bournemouth and lived in Manor Road from 1868 until his death on 2 April 1885. Cairns was Lord Chancellor of England twice, in 1868, and from 1874 to 1880.

The big disappointment, for him and for Bournemouth, was that he had been tipped as Disraeli's successor, but it was not to be. He did, however, make the best political speeches of his time and was acclaimed for a memorable attack on Gladstone's Transvaal policy in 1881.

Among the visitors to Manor Road, in 1872, was his old friend Henry Reeve (1813-95). Credited with having guided the foreign policy of *The Times*, from 1840, he was registrar of the powerful judicial committee of the Privy Council. For four decades he edited the influential *Edinburgh Review*. He discussed with Cairns a project to publish the *Greville Memoirs*.

The Albany, amongst the heights that have been rising since the 1960s, ensures that Manor Road remains exclusive. On the site of Manor Heath and the Steyne, its multi-wing 19-storeys reach more than 200 feet, on top of 100-feet vantage-point foundations. This remains the epitome of life at the seaside with a view instead of a garden.

Opposite the former Adelphi Hotel contrasts with Sandykeld flats

Len to Miss Flo Cave, 4 The Triangle, London W, on 7 December 1904: '**Came down to Bournemouth yesterday. Weather very wet.**'

C.P. to Mrs Tucker, 4 Belvedere, Bath, on 26 May 1905: '**Thank you so much for all the letters you have forwarded. We arrive at Bath at 4.23 on Wednesday 31st. We should be so much obliged if you would open the shutters on that morning. The key of the drawing room door is in the right-hand corner of the left-hand drawer in Mrs P's wardrobe. I hope you will be able to find it.**'

The Albany making its 19-storey statement

ST PETER'S VICARAGE

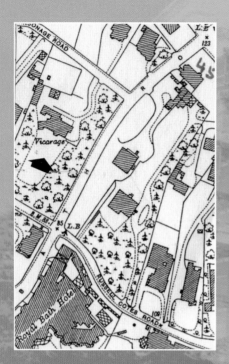

Known originally as the Parsonage, becoming No. 2 Parsonage Road to which it gave its name, the first St Peter's Vicarage was built in 1845-46 on pine-covered ground donated by the Gervis Estate trustees. Standing high above the town's 'Mother Church' it had views across its wide lawn and the bay to the Purbeck Hills. On the south side it faced the Royal Bath Hotel.

The architect, acting for Revd Alexander Morden Bennett, was Edmund Pearce of Canford Magna, Poole. He obtained blocks of mediaeval ashlar and other stone for the cellars from the recently demolished Southampton Castle of which only the Norman vaults remain.

Once a year the lawn became a public space for the whole town. An annual parish party was held on St Peter's Day, which is June 29th. When this fell on a Sunday, 'Entertainments' were postponed until the 30th. The newly-formed Bournemouth Volunteer Rifle Corps first assembled on the Parsonage lawn in 1860 with Charles Allen King of Branksome Dene as its commanding officer and the vicar, Morden Bennett, the chaplain.

Miss Gladys Alexander, this author's mother, was the maid to vicar Revd Lumley Cecil Green-Wilkinson. Aged 17, she arrived with the family from Ascot Heath, Berkshire, in the spring of 1921. By the time they departed in the summer of 1927, she had become the 'eldest' member of Green-Wilkinson's staff.

South view of the Vicarage from its lawn in 1926

The vicarage was sold for £31,000 in 1930 and was then bought by the Prudential Insurance Company, with the extensive site being cleared and replaced by Bath Hill Court flats which were completed in February 1936. This comprises two separate blocks with the southern one being on the site of the lawn.

Future vicars came to regret the decision to move from these rambling Victorian buildings to far-away Inglethorpe at 24 Manor Road. They saw it as an act of madness which absorbed their petrol ration coupons during turbulent times ahead from the outbreak of war in 1939 through to the Suez crisis in 1956. The Manor Road house was sold at auction for £9,050 in 1958. The buildings there were also demolished and replaced by blocks of flats.

The replacement vicarage, at 18 Wimborne Road, had been built for department store proprietor Alderman John Bennett Beale in 1933. It was on the market at £6,350 when the Manor Road property was being sold.

Vicarage maid Gladys Alexander to fiancée Ted Legg at 248 Wimborne Road, Winton, posted from Scotland on 18 August 1926:

> **'Thank you so much for letter. We had a very nice time at the Highland Sports but to-day is raining hard . . . So glad you had a good [motor-cycle] ride. I think [the] men & I are going to the Mill this afternoon. Fondest love, Gladys. [PS] I hope Mrs Weadon is better.'**

(Top left) Bath Hill Court, standing on the Vicarage lawn, from the south in 2008

(Top right) Entrance to Bath Hill Court and its eastern corner, on the site of the Vicarage, in 2008

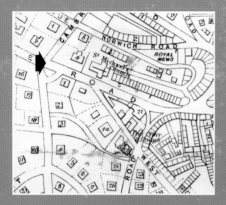

POOLE ROAD

Looking east along the tram-lines towards the Triangle. It is seen from the former cross-roads with Cambridge Road to the north and Durley Chine Road to the south. The pinnacled tower is that of St Michael's Church, added by architect John Oldrid Scott (1842-1913) in 1901. The main building, by Norman Shaw (1831-1912), dates from 1876.

This used to be Bournemouth's Harley Street. The drive emerging to its left is from Hursley, at No. 2 Poole Road, which was the surgery of physician Octavius Carter MD. Opposite, behind the hedge, were physician Alfred Coles MD at York House and ophthalmic surgeon Ernest Maddox MD at Glenartney.

The cross-roads dates from the 1870s when it gave precedence to Poole Road. There were split junctions for both of the side roads. These were laid out spaciously and stylishly, Parisian style, with two facing semi-circles of grass and shrubs. They are now merged into circular St Michael's Roundabout.

Hursley was replaced by a six-storey office block, the Area Office for the Midland Bank, before its take-over by HSBC – the Hong Kong and Shanghai Banking Corporation. Opposite, the Victorian villas have survived, with Laceys Solicitors at No. 5, and Stewarts Accountants on the corner in Glenartney, which is now Ebenezer House.

Just beyond the church, French poet Paul Verlaine (1844-96) had his lodgings above Stirling House, in an apartment above the second shop in 1876-77. He had published his *Romances sans paroles* after running away from his wife and then shooting his next lover, Arthur Rimbauld, in the wrist during a tiff. On leaving prison he fled Paris for Bournemouth and briefly taught classics and his native language at Saint Aloysius College (now 24 Surrey Road). Rimbaud went the other way, to Algiers, to make his fortune as a North African trader.

(Left) *Tram lines towards Poole Hill in the snowstorm of 25 April 1908*

(Right) *Towards Poole Hill, having moved over to glimpse the church tower, in 1908*

The splayed junction, now a roundabout, in 2008

Elsie to Miss Constance Freemantle, The Close, Salisbury, on 7 October 1912: 'We have just returned from a long walk, taking the tram to St Aldhelm's [Church] and walking home. This morning we listened to the band on the pier. We asked Mr Hanson to tea, but received a card saying he could not come today, but would tomorrow and is bringing a clergyman cousin with him . . . We saw Alice in the shop this morning. She waved her hand to us. The sun has been shining all day. We went to St Stephen's last night. Such a nice service [of] Harvest Thanksgiving.'

Stirling House accommodation (above Swinton's in 1995) of gay French poet Paul Verlaine

HORSESHOE COMMON

Horseshoe Common has always been my ideal of public open space. For a start, we proclaimed it as a common and always annoyed bureaucrats, councillors and schoolteachers by asserting that this was Horseshoe Common and the same applied to Redhill Common (which they insisted on calling Redhill Park). Unlike virtually all of them, I was actually born in Bournemouth.

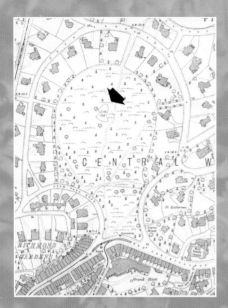

Horseshoe Common, from the pond to the town, in 1912

Commendably greened-up, the view in 2008 defies photography

My evidence was both emotional and practical. Firstly, I had been sent out by my mother with a canvas bag and a wicker basket to collect estovers (twigs in one and pine-cones in the other) from both pieces of ground. Secondly, I heard from an old man in Ripon Road, Moordown (who happened to collect Palaeolithic hand-axes), that Horseshoe Common had its 'Speaker's Corner' where Revd Hugh Wyndham from Salisbury 'fired God's dynamite' by conducting the first religious services in Bournemouth. Thirdly, I felt I had a every right to speak up for both, having gathered a petition to protest against threats to the integrity of Horseshoe Common when road plans were announced in 1960 and joined a repeat protest at Redhill Common.

This Horseshoe, a 'rus in urbe' encircled by Dean Park Road in the 1870s, presents its public face southwards to Old Christchurch Road, midway between the Square and the Lansdowne.

It was never intended that it should remain a green gap as the two acres between the southern ends of Dean Park Crescent and Madeira Road were earmarked for municipal buildings. Even the inner 12 acres only became public in a somewhat hesitant way, being acquired by Bournemouth Corporation from the Dean Estate on a 99-year lease in 1896, at a rent of £5 a year. Most of its older trees were planted early in 1899, including clumps of Californian redwood, Deodar cedar, Maritime pine and Stone pine. The wildest part surrounds the pond which still provides a home for newts and moorhen in the middle of the top curve of the Horseshoe.

Rising ground above the pond used to have a wide view towards the Marine Village, and the tower and spire of St Peter's Church, 500 metres south-west. A century later all is now hidden by scrub at ground level and the tree canopy above. The virtue of the leaves is that they also shroud Wessex Way flyover which for a time compromised the tranquillity of the Horseshoe after it was built from west to east across the centre of the open space in 1961. Now the dual carriageway effectively separates the northern woodland from the southern parkland.

(Left) Amid all this vegetation the pond survives, in 2008

(Right) Even the water appears green, however, apart from a moorhen and chick

MEYRICK PARK

Poor's Common, as it was known, was threatened in 1882 by the London and South Western Railway which attempted to push their line through it. The 'Poor' was not a personal name but the collective one for those who are always with us.

This 'direct line' proposal 'would have completely bisected the common at its prettiest spot' according to the Commons Preservation Society. The scenic centrepiece was known as Marbarrow Valley. Already visualising this as promising 'at no very distant time, to become an open space in the midst of a very large town', the society joined Bournemouth Improvement Commissioners in petitioning against a Parliamentary bill 'and eventually a deviation of the line, as first suggested by the society, was adopted'. This clipped the pine woods on the north side 'in the least objectionable manner'.

Inclosure Allotment No. 62 was then donated to the town for public open space in perpetuity and re-named Meyrick Park for its benefactor, Sir George Eliott Meyrick Tapps-Gervis-Meyrick (1827-1896). The third baronet had succeeded his father at the age of fifteen. In 1883 he surrendered his freehold ownership of this 'turbury common' – shared rights for the removal of peat turves for domestic fuel – to the Bournemouth Improvement Commissioners. 'Gathering firing', as it was called, kept the home fires burning in isolated cottages beside the heath.

Sir George sought no payment for the land but required the commissioners to pledge that it would be kept unenclosed as open space and also incorporate an 18-hole golf links to cater for the new fad that was drawing the middle classes to emerging resorts. These would now include Bournemouth.

Meyrick Park was protected by its own statutory legislation, under the Bournemouth Park Lands Act, 1889 which came into effect on 12 August 1890 and regulated its use 'for the recreation and enjoyment of the public'. The 126 acres of allotment – meaning an open common rather than vegetable plots – was reduced to 118 acres in order to allow small-scale sales of ground to help meet the £13,000 cost of making the park.

Sixty acres were given over to a golf links, with the layout being supervised by early professional Tom Dunn from Tooting Bec, and opened on 28 November 1894 as the first municipal golf course in the country. The line of play of the 18-hole 'Gentlemen's Links' covered

(Left) The big view southwards across Marbarrow Valley on a card posted in 1905

(Right) Great gatherings took place here, such as the Meyrick Park Festival of 23 June 1909

Golfer in one of the few open glimpses available from the same ridge in 2008

two and a quarter miles. There were numerous bunkers and natural obstacles. On the other side of a line of trees was an easy 9-hole 'Ladies' Links' compressed into just half a mile.

The opening ceremony was performed by Sir George's daughter-in-law, Mrs Jacintha Meyrick, of Hinton Admiral. Legal protection for 'the parklands' were carried forward into the Bournemouth Corporation Act, in 1900, which calls for 'the natural aspect and status of the commons' to be preserved.

Major outdoor events have been held here, such as the Bournemouth Centenary celebrations in 1910, and pioneer aviator Gustav Hamel set a 'looping the loop' record over Meyrick Park on 11 April 1914.

A gift of 76 acres by the adjoining Talbot Estate land enabled the extension of the park after the Great War and was dedicated on behalf of the donors by the Earl of Leven and Melville on 15 October 1921.

An annual display by Bournemouth Volunteer Fire Brigade traditionally took place in Meyrick Park. That on 12 September 1923, which attracted 2,000 spectators, marked another couple of the century's changes as it was mechanised, being the first without horses to pull the pumps, and also the first public demonstration of newly-acquired turntable ladders. Ernest R. Whitcome was the pre-war professional at Meyrick Park.

Winton Cricket Club playing Broadstone in July 2008

CRESCENT GARDENS

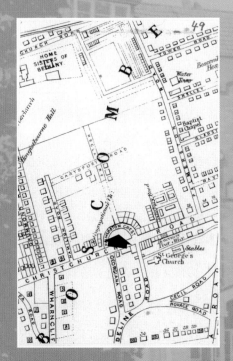

The oldest buildings in this part of Boscombe, on the east side of the junction with Walpole Road, date from 1868 when the crescent was laid out by Sir Henry Drummond Wolff and named Carnarvon Crescent. This was for Wolff's friend Henry Howard Molyneux Herbert, 4th Earl of Carnarvon (1831-90), who was twice Colonial Secretary. It is now known simply as the Crescent but there is a Carnarvon Road only a couple of streets away.

The area was developed as the Palmerston Estate, named for the Prime Minister, Viscount Palmerston, who died in harness in 1866. The former Ragged Cat Inn was rebuilt as the Palmerston Arms. Other roads hereabouts also carry the names of Drummond Wolff's family and friends, particularly those who in 1880 backed his scheme for a freelance 'Fourth Party' in British politics:

Adeline Road (Drummond Wolff's wife, Adeline Sholto Douglas)
Balfour Road (Arthur Balfour, 1st Earl of Balfour, 1848-1930)
Borthwick Road (Algernon Borthwick, 1st Baron Glenesk, 1830-1908)
Cecil Road (Robert Arthur Talbot Gascoyne-Cecil, 3rd Marquis of Salisbury, 1830-1903)
Churchill Road (Lord Randolph Churchill, 1849-1895),
Donoughmore Road (John Luke Hely-Hutchinson, 5th Earl of Donoughmore, 1848-1900)
Gorst Road (Sir John Eldon Gorst, 1835-1916)
Grosvenor Road (Hugh-Lumpus Grosvenor, 1st Duke of Westminster, 1825-99)
Hamilton Road (James Hamilton, 1st Duke of Abercorn, 1811-85)
Randolph Road (see Churchill Road)

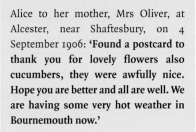

Alice to her mother, Mrs Oliver, at Alcester, near Shaftesbury, on 4 September 1906: **'Found a postcard to thank you for lovely flowers also cucumbers, they were awfully nice. Hope you are better and all are well. We are having some very hot weather in Bournemouth now.'**

Crescent Gardens with the bandstand, in 1913

Orford Road – since renamed Aylesbury
  Road (Robert Horace Walpole, 5th Earl
  of Orford, 1854-1931)
Salisbury Road (see Cecil Road)
Walpole Road (Drummond Wolff's mother,
  Lady Georgiana Walpole)
Wharncliffe Road (Edward Montagu
  Granville Montagu Stuart Wortley
  Mackenzie, 1st Earl of Wharncliffe, 1827-
  99)

Roumelia Lane, dating from 1884,
commemorates Wolff's appointment by the
British Government as a European commissioner for the Turkish province of Eastern
Roumelia – ancient Thrace – during the hiatus
as the Austro-Hungarian empire fell apart.

The eastern side of Crescent Court includes
No. 19, 21, 23, 25 and 27, around to the former
Midland Bank on the corner at No. 504 Christ-
church Road. This now houses six flats.

Crescent Gardens originally had a bandstand. This was replaced by flower-beds. As part
of the most recent changes, Boscombe's former manorial gateposts were brought here as a
display pieces, in a refurbishment opened by the Mayor of Bournemouth, Councillor Dr John
Millward, on 17 September 1994.

*(Top left) Crescent Gardens after removal of
the bandstand, in the 1950s*

*(Top right) Crescent Gardens as a grassy
space, in 2008*

Manorial gatepost brought here in 1994

BOSCOMBE HILL

The view of a bowler-hatted gentleman exchanging greetings with a couple driving a cart towards Bournemouth dates from 1863 and is one of the earliest local photographs. Taken by Robert Day (1822-73), it shows Christchurch Road, looking east, towards Pokesdown and Iford. The Edwardian sequel was photographed by Robert's son, William James Day, who took over the family studio beside the original Scotch Church in the Square, at the foot of Richmond Hill, on the site of the Empress Hotel.

Christchurch Road on Boscombe Hill was the dividing line between Bournemouth and Boscombe. The magazine *Vanity Fair* reported in October 1875 that:

> '...separated only by a small ravine from the last house in Bournemouth proper is another rising collection of villas surrounding an architecturally picturesque hotel of goodly size and accommodation. This infant place is known by the name of Boscombe Spa ... Boscombe is a pretty little place somewhat bare at present.'

Then and now, 1863 and 1910

To the right are Boscombe Gardens which were laid out by Sir Henry Drummond Wolff MP in 1868. Since 1908 there have been formal flower beds in a rotation which is changed twice a year. Ross Young, as Bournemouth's parks director, introduced mini-golf in 1967 and devised three-dimensional floral displays, notably of an Owl and Thomas the Tank Engine.

(Next page) Updated to 2008

Driver and carriage passing the Royal
Arcade towards the Grand in the 1898

Driver and carriage passing the Royal Arcade towards the Grand in the 1898

ROYAL ARCADE

Five commercial projects transformed the centre of Victorian Boscombe along the north side of Christchurch Road. Entrepreneur Archibald Beckett (1842-1904) from Tisbury masterminded the scheme after having overcome legal hassles such as the removal of covenants on numerous plots of land which had restricted all development to residential housing.

Firstly, in 1889, the Colonnade block was built on the corner of Christchurch Road and Palmerston Road. Secondly, in 1890, the 35-bedroom Salisbury Hotel opened on the site of Dunston Villa, towards Ashley Road.

Thirdly, in 1892, the Royal Arcade was built from the west side of Salisbury Hotel, around the back of the Colonnade, and into Palmerston Road. Opening in August that year, it not only boasted a glass canopy, but was also lit by electricity. Concert parties, a choral society, and an

organ soloist provided varied light music to put a skip into shoppers' steps. A somewhat retrospective official opening took place on 19 December 1892 when Queen Victoria's third son, His Royal Highness Prince Arthur, Duke of Connaught (1850-1942) visited Bournemouth. Among those who met him were the architectural partnership of Lawson and Donkin.

Fourthly, came a range of shops and offices under the name Boscombe Chambers.

Fifthly and finally, behind the block, there was the Grand which was one of the biggest theatres on the South Coast. Covering 15,000 square feet, with an auditorium rising 50 feet, the stage was also of enormous proportions – 44 feet wide by 40 feet deep – to cater for a wide range of productions from comedies to musicals. Work started in March 1894 and cost £15,500. The opening day was 17 May 1895. It became Boscombe Hippodrome music hall in 1905 and is still in business as the Opera House.

Entrance to the Royal Arcade, 2008

J.M.W. to Mrs Taylor, at 47 Turnpike Road, Hornsey, on 26 April 1910: **'Sorry you have not a maid, do not know one to suit you. Thank you for all books, papers & letters. All well.'**

Nancy to Mrs Brockway, Railway Cottage, West Moors, Dorset, in the reign of George V: **'Dear People, We shall be very pleased to see you all on Thursday. Bob expects to be away all day tomorrow (Wed). Hope you will bring fine weather.'**

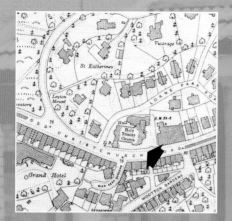

HOLY TRINITY CHURCH

Robert Kerley, chairman of Bournemouth Improvement Commissioners in 1867, who had been a churchwarden at St Peter's – the 'Mother Church' of Bournemouth – a decade earlier, donated land at Madeira Vale for the building of a second town-centre church. His motivation was to counter-balance the Oxford-inspired High Church movement which was taking Bournemouth under its wing.

The alternative Low Church place of Anglican worship was built in Lombardy Gothic style by Carlisle architect Charles J. Ferguson. Brick and terracotta were chosen to contrast with the traditional stone of other churches. 'Glory to God in the highest' ran poster-sized capital letters in the semi-circular apse behind the altar.

Dedicated to the Holy Trinity, its foundation stone was laid on 2 June 1868 by the 'tall and handsome' philanthropist Antony Ashley Cooper, 7th Earl of Shaftesbury. It was a big building, cruciform in shape, with 'a spacious and lofty' nave 90 feet long, 30 feet wide, and 45 feet high. On either side, the transepts were 20 feet deep, 24 feet wide, and 33 feet high. Over a thousand worshippers could be accommodated.

The bell-tower was particularly noticeable both in being detached from the main building and being built on a sloping plinth which then rose 80 feet perpendicularly.

The church was consecrated on 28 September 1869, by Right Revd Vincent William Ryan, the evangelical former Bishop of Mauritius. The two Bournemouth congregations mingled in the

Holy Trinity, with its detached tower, and Cumnor House, in a view posted in 1906

(Next page) The Trinity development and Bar Vin in 2008

Holy Trinity Church, Bournemouth

J.W.S. 1868.

Cumnor House, around the back of Bar Vin, in 2008

street as they made their way along Old Christchurch Road. Those attending St Peter's carried the Book of Common Prayer and a hymn book. Holy Trinity communicants brandished a bible.

Its first vicar, Revd. Philip Eliot (1835-1917), left Bournemouth for Winchester Cathedral in 1890 and became Dean of Windsor. He was domestic chaplain to Queen Victoria and King Edward VII. One of his regular communicants at Holy Trinity was the hydrographer Admiral Sir James Sulivan (1810-90) who sailed with Charles Darwin on the famous voyage of the *Beagle*. The father of the first British subject to be born on the Falkland Islands – Falkland Sulivan – Sir James lived at Tregew (the 25-27 Gervis Road site which became the Anglo-Swiss Hotel). He introduced a young friend, 16-year-old Beatrice Potter, to the church in 1875. She was confirmed there. The future Mrs Sidney Webb was attending Stirling House finishing school at the top of Bath Hill. Later, as a Fabian socialist, she had second thoughts:

'I see now the year I spent in Bournemouth I was vainly trying to smother my instinct of truth in clinging to the old faith.'

Holy Trinity's Edwardian vicar was Rev A. S. V. Blunt, the father of art connoisseur and traitor and onetime knight Professor Sir Anthony Blunt. Anthony was born in the vicarage above the church, at 16 Madeira Road, on 26 September 1907. Young Blunt became one of the Cambridge Apostles in the 1930s, spied for the Soviets throughout the Second World War, and after the defection of Guy Burgess and Donald Maclean tipped off third-man Kim Philby, who fled to join them in Russia.

Blunt was also a leading international art expert. Rewarded with a knighthood as surveyor of the Queen's Pictures in 1956, he was grilled by MI5, but allowed to retain his freedom and status until publicly unmasked, in a statement to the House of Commons, by Prime Minister Margaret Thatcher in 1979. As a result he was stripped of his title. Unrepentant, he died in 1983.

Holy Trinity was declared redundant and demolished in the 1980s. The site has since been redeveloped in two blocks which are named Trinity. Current occupants include CMA Recruitment Group, Robert Half International, Unit World 2 School of English, National Cosmetic Centres, National Slimming Centres and NMC Property. Cumnor House, behind what is now Bar Vin, has survived. It is remembered for having housed the Model Railway Museum.

Lou to Mrs Phillpotts, Woodland Leigh, Spring Gardens, Swindon, on 3 September 1904: **'We are all very well & enjoying ourselves. Babe is very good indeed. Mrs I's son who is ill is the leading boy in the choir at this church. He is making satisfactory progress.'**

'D' to Miss Thompson in Bath Road, Frome, Somerset, on 16 December 1925: **'I am afraid I shall miss S. school again next Sunday, as we have decided to stay here till Monday. The vicar is better but if he does not take services on Sunday, there will be a better chance for Xmas.'**

Edwin Dodshon photographed the laying
of a commemorative stone on 8 July 1929

Two o'clock Sun-time (GMT not BST) on a
July afternoon in 2008

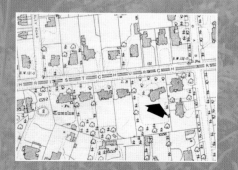

BOURNEMOUTH
NATURAL SCIENCE SOCIETY

The plot at No. 39 Christchurch Road was bought by businessman and churchwarden John Cassels in 1878. He commissioned architect Henry Joy, who built Westbourne Arcade, to design Bassendean as his home in 1879. Cassels moved into the villa in 1880. Contemporary maps show that at about this position, set back from the south side of the road, there was a large 'Tumulus' – a Bronze Age round barrow burial mound – which was levelled during building work and is now under this or the next-door garden.

In 1919, Bassendean was bought by Bournemouth Natural Science Society, and refurbished by 1923 as its lecture hall, library, offices and accommodation. Founded in 1883, and re-formed in 1903, it began with eight sections, each with its own chairman – Archaeological & Historical, Botanical, Geographical, geological, Microscopical, Photographical, Physical and Zoological. Summer field excursions and winter meetings attracted the town's intellectual elite. Many donated their collections, ranging from fossils and shells to butterflies and stuffed birds. Before the Great War, an average of 75 meetings were held each year.

The picture shows the unveiling of a commemorative stone set in the wall of its half-built extension. This reads:

> **'Laid by Sir Daniel Morris K.C.M.G., D.Sc., D.C.L., LL.D, F.L.S. Past-President. July 8th 1929.'**

Except that he never laid it, resident caretaker Steven Moult told me, and curator John Cresswell provided other details. Sir Daniel Morris (1844-1933) was unwell. As the 85-year-old agricultural botanist languished at home – 14 Crabton Close, Boscombe – Lady Margaret Morris deputised for the day.

The building also provided rooms for Bournemouth & District Blind Aid Society Lending Library, the Bournemouth Medical Society, and the Hants & Dorset Branch of the Royal Empire Society.

(Bottom left) The house and hall from the grounds, 2008

(Bottom right) Stuffed birds lining the hall, 1973

(Top left) *Charminster House in a view posted in 1904*

(Top right) *Almost from the same spot (cars were in the way) in 2008*

Queen's Park and its pond on early colour film, 1937

Next page: Less heather, more trees, in 2008

CHARMINSTER (and Queen's Park)

Charminster House stands on the east side of Charminster Road at the corner with Malmesbury Park Road. It was number 36 Charminster Road in the time of wine merchant Walter B. Dell. Then it was split into two shops with the two windows to the right being the shop of provisions grocer Charles Wyndham Phillips. Applegates were the next wine and spirits merchants to occupy the corner.

The shop-fronts were extended forwards and in the process have erased or hidden the Christchurch House plaque as well as the bottom layers of its brickwork corner-piece.

Enough bricks remain, however, for this distinctive feature to confirm our identification. Re-numbered as 74 Charminster Road, in postcode BH8 8UR, it is again re-united as a single large off-licence with the shop being run by Thresher Wine Merchants, a national company with headquarters at Enjoyment Hall, Bessemer Road, Welwyn Garden City, Hertfordshire AL7 1BL. Sales assistant Leigh Faulkner stood in the doorway for me, in July 2008, on his predecessor's steps.

Queen's Park

Golf Course

From Tip Hill to Littledown Drive, in 1936

Walter to Brice Dell in Cresswell Grove, West Didsbury, Manchester, on 30 August 1904: **'How's the world using you? Got over your holidays? Weather here is perfect. Dear M & Lou coming on Thursday for a few days. Lil & family A1.'**

Charminster's green lung is Queen's Park. The lost name here is Tip Hill, where the clubhouse now stands beside Holdenhurst Road, was named for a disused two-acre gravel pit which became one of the town's first open tips. Work started on the public park and its 18-hole golf links when John Elmes Beale was mayor, from 1902 to 1905. The landscape is a rolling mix of pine plantations and relict heathland.

Bournemouth Inclosure Commissioners had awarded allotments No. 59 and 60 as Poor's Commons for the people. Tip Hill, beside Holdenhurst Road, was the site of the town's refuse destructor. Bournemouth Corporation used its legal powers to convert allotment No. 60 into Queen's Park, on the north side of Holdenhurst Road, and King's Park on the south side formed a smaller part of No. 59. The latter, being flat and next to

Hidden in the middle distance is a main road, in 2008

artisan Boscombe, was largely given over to sports grounds. Beside them, 35 acres had already been turned into the East Cemetery, in 1891.

The park plans ran into legal difficulties, however, until 9 April 1900 when Mr Justice Chambers, sitting in the High Court, released landowner Sir George Meyrick to sell the land. The monarchs that councillors had in mind in naming King's Park (86 acres) and Queen's Park (173 acres) were King Edward VII and Queen Alexandra.

Queen's Park Drive (now Queen's Park Avenue) was opened on 26 September 1906. The professional at the golf course between the wars was Don Curtis.

The new Ringwood Spur Road, via Cooper Dean roundabout, emptied into a high-speed Holdenhurst Road, which was widened into Queen's Park in the late 1960s. This was known officially as 'Holdenhurst Road Relief Road, Phase I' and took Wessex Way dual carriageway, to Queen's Park Roundabout. Phase II, in 1973, pushed on westwards to link up with the next completed length of Wessex Way at Methuen Road in 1975.

Evelyn to Mrs W. J. King, 41 Trelawney Road, Plymouth, on 30 April 1926: **'We are having a very good time & Mother seems much better for the change. We come back to Plymouth on Monday. I have been trying to play golf, not very successfully. The weather is quite nice but rather uncertain.'**

HOLDENHURST

The riverside village of Holdenhurst pre-dates the Victorian new town of Bournemouth by more than a thousand years. Christchurch, in Norman times, included the liberty of Westover, part of which was the manor of Holeest (Holdenhurst). Until 1839, the hamlet had a surviving Saxon chapel and for more than another century a fine collection of rustic buildings that looked as if they were a million miles from the conurbation when soldiers of the 11th Infantry Brigade,

Holdenhurst Farm with the 5th Battalion, Northamptonshire Regiment, on manoeuvres in 1940

recently returned from Dunkirk in 1940, invaded it on manoeuvres. They prepared to fight the Germans on the beaches, through the town, and into the meadows of the River Stour.

Much of this green idyll lingered on in tranquil decay until triple whammies in the 1970s. These were the building of new A338 'Spur Road' dual carriageway from Ringwood to Bournemouth – sweeping beside Townsend Cottages – and the construction of a huge sewage works when it became environmentally unacceptable to dump untreated excrement into the sea.

Holdenhurst Farm, the thatched back-drop to the wartime photograph, has been demolished. Riverside Avenue, cut by the new road, is now a couple of cul-de-sacs, with the length from Iford serving as a rear access to a care home, law court and a supermarket.

Reminders that the 'Parish of Holdenhurst' previously stretched from the river to the sea – giving it the status of the mother parish of Bournemouth town – survive as tablets of stone deep in the modern conurbation.

From Townsend to Riverside Avenue in about 1910

Townsend is a little busier in 2008

This is A338 at Holdenhurst, in 2008, so do use the bridge?

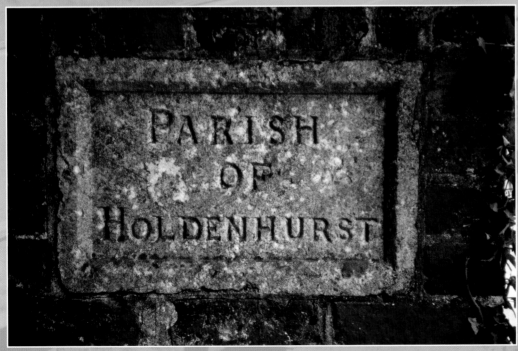

Boundary stone, in Talbot Road, 2000

PARISH OF HOLDENHURST

Play-place shallows in the 1920s

Whooper swan, wintering here on the Stour, shot 20 January 1891

(Next page) Deep-waters now for contemplative members of the next generation, 2008

PIG SHUTE

Remembered as a wide, open gravel track to the river-bank, this access point has shrunk into a leafy path. Historically, it was a droveway for watering stock in the River Stour, from Holdenhurst and Throop. The waterside was well-trod and muddy. On the other side, 150 metres downstream via the shallows, Pig Shute Lane was the public road to West Hurn, passing Hurn Court (known for a time as Heron Court), its parkland and the field with the Earl of Malmesbury's ice-house.

The river can still be reached but paddling is now out of the question.

By the 1950s a concrete retaining wall had been built to prevent further erosion. As a result, scouring around the outer edge of this long curve has been downwards, rather than outwards. The effect has turned these former shallows into one of the deepest parts of the Stour, which is said to be 14 feet deep.

On the riverbank I found Charles Galloway from Castle Point, Strouden Park, fishing for perch in July 2008. Any catch is put back. A quiet watcher, he had recently notched up sightings of kingfishers, foxes, mink and roe deer.

(Left) Punt and rope Riddlesford Ferry was still in use in the 1920s

(Right) Another shot by amateur photographer Edwin Dodshon in the 1920s

RIDDLESFORD

The ancient crossing point at 'Redylesford' was by a punt ferry with the course of the craft being controlled by a rope. There was also a ford for carts and stock, at the historic point where until 1930 (to the south) and 1974 (to the north), the Dorset Stour became a Hampshire river. Southwards, the track through the valley bottom at Redhill Common became Boundary Lane and led to Parkstone and Branksome Dene. Produce from the coast included contraband liquor, copperas, fish and salt. Cattle were brought in the opposite direction.

Revd Alexander Sykes Bennett, a deacon from Wilton, returned home to Bournemouth in 1863 to help his father, the vicar of Bournemouth, to run mission churches in the Hampshire-Dorset borderlands. He regularly rode to Red Hill, dismounted, and took the Riddlesford ferry, to walk across the meadows to take services at East Parley.

The public bridleway continued to lead to the river – between fences – but the ferry point went with Riverside and became a lawnside attraction for Marshall's Tea and Strawberry Gardens at Riverside from Edwardian times through to the 1930s. Charles Marshall (1843-1908) and his wife, Love Lawford (1843-1921) opened the business in 1903. Their youngest son, Pascoe Marshall (1886-1958) remembered the August bank holiday at the start of the Great War, in 1914, for their busiest-ever day:

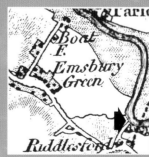

This was the spot but the river has been
moved away from Redhill Park Homes,
2008

'That Saturday was the busiest day I had ever known. In separate teapots I made tea
for 300 people. By standing at the hot-water tap for three hours I developed knee
trouble which later turned into synovitis. This bothered me for a long time but it
probably stopped me getting into worse trouble as it made me unfit for soldiering.'

One of his elder brothers, Major Harold Marshall MC (1870-1918), died as a result of having
been gassed. Harold had been the boating enthusiast. Then there was a double tragedy. Two
young ladies, daughters of Mrs Green who was the schoolmistress at East Parley, were taken
across by the ferry one foggy night. The ferryman, Charles Corbin, told them to strike off across
the fields to their home, but they never arrived. Footsteps found in the morning showed they
had slipped on the muddy bank. Their bodies were found later. Perhaps because of this, Pascoe
Marshall insisted that the ferry was an 'obligement', rather than a legal service:

'The river at the tea garden was at times quite swift and to use the ferry-boat with a
punt-pole was quite a work of art, especially as we were supposed to land at one
certain spot on the opposite bank.'

Usage of the ford is said to have ceased as a result of stronger currents which followed
construction of the New Road causeway and bridge, upstream from Northbourne to Parley Cross,
in 1910. The name was preserved by a house name, William Harman's Ruddleford, which had

become Ruddiford when Ronald Legg was living there in the 1960s. I was told that 'riddle' and 'ruddle' had the same origin as 'reddle' or 'ruddle' for red ochre – the pigment – that was used to mark sheep. It could have been made here, from heathland exposures of clay and haematic iron oxide, and taken and to farms by reddlemen.

The river itself has been shifted northwards, to prevent it from further undermining the sandy slopes at Redhill which were still literally a 'Red Hill' – its older name – with exposed strata until the road system was overhauled in the 1960s. Older residents described a 'red gravel face of some fifty feet'.

The old ferry point now lies under the most northerly of the caravans that comprise Redhill Park Homes. Above them are Wheatplot Park Homes, numbers 1 to 17. Wheatplot used to be a strawberry field. The Marshall family owned about two acres of these slopes.

There is now public access around each side of the caravan sites. Clockwise, begin beside bungalow No. 1213 Wimborne Road and follow the pavement westwards as it descends to a subway. Now turn right, along the path northwards, into Stour Valley local nature reserve. Keep bearing right until you reach a fishing pontoon and then walk up the path to return to the cul-de-sac length of old main road at Edgehill Cottage.

Pascoe Marshall was wrong when he mused 'that the track itself is, I suppose, lost to public use for ever'.

The Stour with 'Chris R' casting for pike, perch and chub in July 2008

(Left) Present bridge in the course of construction, 1905

(Right) From the north side, with a tram heading for Christchurch, circa 1912

TUCKTON BRIDGE

Historically, there were only two road crossings of the River Stour in the vicinity of Bournemouth as it emerged into a Victorian new town. The first up from the sea, in three miles, was Iford Bridge, and it was another six miles to the next, which was Longham Bridge.

Projects for intermediate crossing points started with that for Tuckton Bridge, which was first promoted at a Town Hall meeting in Christchurch on 18 March 1875. Models were made and quotations obtained. A wooden and iron combination was estimated at between £1,800 (18 feet wide) or £2,300 (21 feet wide) plus £100 for the approaches. The principal proponent was Christchurch Mayor Nicholas Sambrooke Newlyn who had a vested interest in an improved route to Bournemouth as he owned the Exeter Hotel.

Tuckton Bridge Company held its first meeting on 25 April 1882. To designs by T. Stevens, at a total cost of £3,921-6s.-1d., the bridge opened in May 1883. Through tolls, of a penny for a pedestrian up to sixpence for a four-wheeled carriage, the company achieved its objective of a five per cent return on its capital.

The need for a replacement was to embrace the next century's first and foremost form of road transport which was the tram rather than the motor car. This became possible when the Borough of Bournemouth absorbed Southbourne in 1904. The first tram ran across, into Christchurch, on 17 October 1905. Profits now went to the ratepayer – who paid most of them in the first place – with a net total of £40,000 between then and the eventual abolition of toll charges in 1943. The toll house, at the north-west corner, was removed and its site is now overgrown with scrub. Its sign also disappeared:

'Traction Engines must not cross the Bridge.'

As for other bridging points, Ensbury Bridge was built in 1910 to carry the New Road from Northbourne to Parley Cross. Next and last, in the late 1960s, was the project for the A338 Spur Road from Ringwood though its actual crossing – upstream from former Blackwater Ferry – is in the parish of Hurn.

From the beer garden of the Harvester Riverside Inn, 2008

Detail of the cast iron parapet, 2008

The bridge emphatically belongs to Bournemouth, 2008

Rights of passage applying to the water as well, 2008

WICK FERRY

The lowest crossing point on the River Stour, Wick Ferry was of considerable commercial importance before the building of Tuckton Bridge, before which the first fixed crossing was Iford Bridge. Wick Ferry was the direct route from Christchurch town to outlying parts of its parish from Pokesdown and Tuckton to the emergent Southbourne-on-Sea.

Proponents of the Tuckton bridging project carried out a traffic census over the winter and spring of 1880-81 which showed an average of 97 carriages, 5 wagons and 17 pack-horses crossing two miles upstream at Iford Bridge every day. Usage of Wick ferry, a service for pedestrians only, totalled 228 adults and 85 children a day.

Blackberry Lane was the name of the track directly towards the sea, passing Clark's Farm, to Cellarfield Farm and the Cellars on the cliff. The vintage ancient road, however, was that from Tuckton to Hengistbury Head – still a dusty path in places to this day – which was a continuation of Castle Lane and Iford Lane and linked the Stour Valley with its principal Iron Age port, on the shore of Christchurch Harbour beyond Wick Hams.

Just around the corner from Wick ferry, lived one of the heroes of our time. A printer's son, Acting Sergeant George Eardley (1912-91) retired to 29 Branders Lane. He won the Victoria Cross for a daring and virtually suicidal one-man dash against strongly-held German positions in orchards east of Overloon, Belgium, on 16 October 1944. Ignoring withering fire, with his Sten-gun and grenades, he killed all the enemy soldiers in three machine-gun posts. He also held the

(Previous page) Wick Ferry from the water in 1902

Land view, towards Christchurch, in 1913

Military Medal for a feint in Normandy in which he pretended to be wounded as he crept towards a position which he then destroyed. His reward at a Buckingham Palace investiture was two glasses of sherry with King George VI who was delighted that for once the recipient of the VC was still alive.

An electrical engineer for Rolls-Royce, the course of George Eardley's life was changed by an horrific peacetime accident at Nantwich, in June 1964. His wife, Winifred, was killed by a train as they drove through a malfunctioning level-crossing. George's foot was cut free without anaesthetic. His second marriage was to Nancy Barrett, who had been his teenage sweetheart, whom he brought to Wick Village.

Boats have been traditionally available at both Tuckton and Wick, at 6d per hour in 1891. In recent times most of the business has come from the Christchurch side of the water where Christchurch Rowing Club was founded in 1948 and Fred Pontin established what is now described as a 'Holiday Facility'. As camp came into fashion the word fell out of use. Today, the main honeypot is still the other side, in the guise of the Captain Club Hotel.

The present-day ferryman is Tony Lo Nigro and his fare in 2008 was 70p for a return ticket (or 40p if you wish to stay in Christchurch). There are two crossing points. One, at the corner of Wick Lane beside Riverside, is a public slipway. There used to be a hut here for the ferryman. A few yards upstream, in the bushes, is the timber quay from which the ferry now operates.

Con & George to Mr and Mrs Tye, 6 Stanley Terrace, Devizes, Wiltshire, on 8 July 1953: **'Having a nice time. Weather could be better. The girls are enjoying themselves. We have been to Boscombe & Christchurch today. This is an ideal spot here.'**

The ferryman, Tony Lo Nigro, with his passengers, July 2008

There is also a public slipway at Wick Ferry, 2008

TALBOT VILLAGE

Two spinster sisters, Georgina Charlotte Talbot and Mary Anne (alternatively Marianne) Talbot, were daughters and heiresses of Sir George Talbot of Mickleham, Surrey, who was directly descended from the 1st Earl of Shaftesbury. On their mother's side they inherited a powerful mix of Irish and Scottish ancestry including, in alphabetical order, the families of the Earl of Arran, Viscount Boyne, Robert the Bruce, Dawson, Preston, Tighe, and the Earls of Winton and Edington. With the death of Sir George, on 10 June 1850, the Talbot baronetcy became extinct. His daughters found themselves owning prime pieces of London from Grosvenor Square and Kensington to the Portobello Farm Estate. Sales between 1852 and 1862 raised £150,000 which was put towards building Talbot Village.

Social problems concerned the ladies. Landless labourers found their cash from poaching and smuggling. Mary Anne Talbot described protests against poverty:

> **'All around the neighbourhood the distress and suffering of the poor was dreadful. The people used to come in crowds, calling out "Give us work, give us work – we are starving!" Men, women and children came in alarming numbers with spades and sticks, under the windows – and the few sovereigns given away did more harm than good.'**

The answer to this, from the sister, was very Samuel Smiles, along the lines of his *Self Help* treatise. As they sold their London inheritance, the sisters bought 465 acres on the Dorset-Hampshire borderlands. They sub-divided the land between five farms and 16 cottages. Each cottage was allocated an acre of land and a pigsty. It was the agricultural answer to Robert Owen's industrial community at New Lanark in Scotland. Talbot Village was then in Dorset, in the parish of Kinson, and no persons from Hampshire were allowed to live there. This restriction was intended to exclude itinerants who were attracted to the adjacent new town of Bournemouth.

By 1861 there was a range of almshouses, designed by Christopher Crabbe Creeke, to cater for those no longer able to work their land. The school followed in 1862 for the other end of the demographics. St Mark's Church was to completed the picture. Miss Georgina Talbot laid the foundation stone on 12 May 1868 and it was built at a cost of £5,000, in Purbeck and Portland stone, by Evans & Fletcher from Wimborne to designs by Walter Fletcher. Its special treasure is a Roman white marble fountain-size vase, four feet high and three feet in diameter, from the River Tiber. This was brought to England from Rome by Sir George Talbot. It is now the font.

Georgina Talbot died only days before the first service at St Mark's, on 19 February 1870, after a short illness and was the first to be buried in its churchyard:

> **'. . . the remains of this benevolent and beneficent founder of the village were deposited in her vault on the day succeeding its consecration.'**

Mary Anne Talbot continued the work until her death in 1885. Her additions carry the initials 'MT'. Their work was being taken up on the grand scale by soap magnate William Hesketh Lever at Port Sunlight and the chocolate-making Rowntree family at Bourneville. Mary Anne mused:

Alice to Mrs Oliver, South View, Alcester, near Shaftesbury, on 28 September 1906: 'Dear Mother, Thank you so much for nice card. Hope you are better. I am well now and went to Boscombe last week. They are all well up there.'

F.L.U. to Mrs Nellie Freak, Shepherd's Corner, Durweston, near Blandford, on 26 July 1908: 'Just a card to say I got back quite safe but feel rather dull & tired after all my lively times I had with you especially on Friday night. I have not forgot that & I do think it is a very good photo of it. Will you thank him very much. I am delighted with it. Can't stop to say more. Will write in the week.'

(Top left) Entrance gates to Talbot Village from Wallisdown Road in 1907

(Top right) Entrance to Talbot Village from the University Roundabout, 2008

(Bottom left) Hedgerow sign on the corner of Wallisdown Road and Alton Road, 2008

(Bottom right) Lavender Cottage in 2008

Entrance to Talbot Woods Bournemouth

TALBOT VILLAGE

'E. & M.' to Mrs Hill, Bourneville, 10 Surrey Road South, Bournemouth, on 13 February 1917: 'Birmingham Station. My Dear, We reached here safely just before 3. Not at all a bad journey – in fact a very warm one. Had some sandwiches at Gloucester – have just had some more & sampled the contents of the flask. Delicious! Very many thanks to you all for every thing. We had a lovely time with you all. Keep well & come and see us soon.'

G. Hole, staying at Rochester, West Hill Road, Bournemouth W, to Mr D. Dallon on 11 September 1917: ' The weather so far has been exceptionally fine & I am feeling better for the change & rest. I trust you are quite well & that the trying events in London have not disturbed you.'

Irene to Mrs M. M. Stapleton in Brook Barn Way, Worthing, on 2 November 1943: 'Had a grand run down. No mishaps at all. Called at Joan's, Emsworth. They have a nice bungalow there . . . Went to a service after supper. Met a few friends of last year but visitors not so many now. Posting this on way to church. Thought of you and hoped you did not feel too lonely after the car turned the corner. Cheerio.'

Professor Asa Briggs, vice-chancellor of Sussex University, about Talbot Village in 1972: 'It seems to me pre-eminently worth preserving and I would gladly add my name to those of others in an effort to have it declared an area of historical interest.'

'It has been difficult to find a name for this Institution for the Agricultural classes. It cannot be called an Asylum because the cottagers may be sent away but it may be termed a Model Village created on the principles of Christian Charity and kindness.'

Her heir, Ronald Ruthven Melville, added further land in 1890 and built Talbot Manor as a memorial to Mary Anne Talbot. This was given to the Society for Waifs and Strays – destitute boys – which became the Church of England Society, now administered through the Shaftesbury Society. The Talbot family home, Hinton Wood House, was at 11 Grove Road, on the East Cliff. Talbot Village survives substantially intact. A few cottages have been demolished, however,

Lulworth in 2008

including that at its entrance. All seemed to be endangered in 1973 when Bournemouth & District Civic Society persuaded the public and the trustees that it was their moral duty to preserve this rare example of a philanthropic model village as a tribute to Victorian altruism. In the process they have also preserved Bournemouth's last full-sized pine wood as the backdrop to 'arcadia in suburbia'.

Much of the surrounding land has been sold. Modern housing and the campus of Bournemouth University now occupy the former open pastures on the other side of Wallisdown Road. School playing fields form a buffer zone to the north.

The *Bournemouth Graphic* in 1905:

'The cottages are overgrown with Virginia creeper, jessamine and honeysuckle. These surroundings give a restful feeling. One thinks of Gray's *Elegy*. It might as easily have been written in Talbot churchyard as Stoke Poges.'

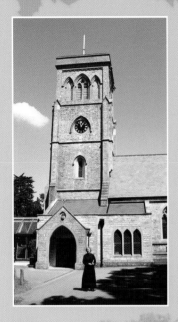

(Top left) St Mark's Church with assistant curate Revd Phyllis Jones in 2008

(Top centre left) The Roman fountain that is now a font, 2008

(Top centre right) Scot's pine flanking the main path though Talbot Woods, in a view posted in 1908

(Top right)
The same path, plus a foxglove, in 2008

(Bottom)
Typical cottage in the trees, 2008

THE MODERNE

Built in the early 1930s, the Moderne Cinema had a cramped frontage that took the place of a couple of terraced houses at Nos. 711 to 715 Wimborne Road, on the east side of the main road through Moordown. The flamboyant facade conceals an enormous fortress-like blockhouse of white brick – the cheapest and least durable product of the West Howe brickfields – which, with its car-park, cover a huge L-shaped plot from Balfour Road in the north to Brassey Road in the south. Balfour Road was named for Major Kenneth Robert Balfour, the constituency's Conservative MP from 1900 to 1906. Brassey Road, for political balance, was in honour of his Liberal opponent, Captain the Honourable Thomas Allnutt Brassey, 1st Earl Brassey.

The dimensions of the main building were considerable – the ground floor of the cinema comprised 13,500 cubic feet; upper foyer level 4,915 cubic feet; circle level 7,473 cubic feet; and the projection suite 1,252 square feet.

There were shops beside the entrance-way, with Ashley Wallpapers on the south side, and estate agents Blake & Bailey to the north. The remainder of the terrace, to Balfour Road, incorporated three shops, of the Home Bakery pastrycooks at No. 717, watch-maker Norman Dey at No. 719, and J. Jordan's café at No. 721. Jeweller and goldsmith A. W. Lucas then took over Nos. 717 and 719 as a single shop.

In my time of attending here the Moderne Cinema was owned by Portsmouth Town Cinemas Ltd. The films I recall seeing here, still in vivid detail, were *The Battle of the River Plate*, the *Cockleshell Heroes*, *Reach for the Sky*, *The Dam Busters*, *Dunkirk*, *The Colditz Story*, *The Bridge on the River Kwai*, *The Colditz Story* and *The Yangtse Incident*. That places my childhood, and fascination for military history, to the mid-1950s. I also enjoyed Ealing comedies and went on to see the whole St Trinian's series. There were some 'Cowboys', but only adult screenings, as I could not stand the screaming crèche that was Saturday morning cinema.

Beside the entrance to the Moderne – each first week of November – I went begging, with my contemporary Norman Chislett. Our mobile 'Penny for the Guy' display was transported on a go-cart. Half-crowns from Teddy Boys represented unprecedented wealth to a couple of working class kids.

My interest in the building ceased when this became one of the first cinemas to convert into a bingo hall, following the liberalisation of gambling laws, in 1961. That form of pleasure

(Top) The Moderne Cinema after its conversion to Bingo in 1960

(Bottom) On the market in 2008

was for our mothers and aunts. It continued to operate as Gala Bingo into recent times but by 2008 had been put on the market. The agents were Edward Flude and Phillip Hartley at Flude Commercial. It was advertised as being classified 'D2 (Assembly and Leisure) under the Town & Country Planning (Classes Order) 1987' with 'potential for redeveloping the land to the rear of the shops fronting Wimborne Road'.

(Top, left) Side view of the fortress-like auditorium, 2008

(Top right) Balfour Road, which was named for a local MP, rather than the Prime Minister, 2008

(Bottom) Views inside courtesy the Flude Commercial web-site, 2008

The Cemetery — Bournemouth

(Left) *The entrance and its Lodge, on a card posted in 1905*

(Right) *Replacement caretaker's house but otherwise much the same in 2008*

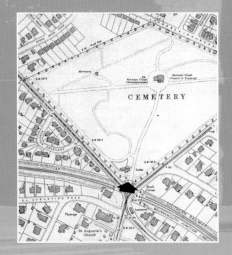

CEMETERY

WIMBORNE ROAD CEMETERY

Opened as the 'New Cemetery' beside Rush Corner, which soon became known as Cemetery Junction, between Wimborne Road and Charminster Road, this was established by a burial board of the parishes of St Peter's and Holy Trinity which was formed in 1872. Its main avenue features golden hollies alternating with *Araucaria araucana* or Chile pine. Commonly known as the monkey-puzzle – for its close-set prickly leaves – this had been introduced in 1795 and became highly fashionable in Victorian times.

The entrance, at 124 feet above sea level, faces Richmond Hill and St Augustin's Church. Consecrated on 28 October 1892, this was provided by hymn writer Canon Henry Twells who retired from Waltham to Thornleigh in Bodorgan Road. A self-confessed 'Bournemouth grumbler' he campaigned through local verses such as 'Don't cut down the pines'.

The cemetery's planting scheme was the idea of Joseph Cutler who personally intervened to prevent laurels being added to the mix, as he explained in April 1877:

> **'I beg to inform the public that there were no shrubs stolen from the New Cemetery but it was unanimously agreed by the burial board that there should be no laurels planted in the cemetery. One morning I discovered 50 of these ugly and poisonous plants. I enquired, but could not find out who had them planted, and not finding them in Mr Stewart's bill (the contractor for the shrubs), I, being a member of the board and on the committees of planting and building, I took them up and threw them away. I would just say that anything done on the cemetery ground without the sanction of the board will doubtless meet with the same fate.'**

Many of the money puzzles survive but the original railings around the perimeter walls were

Tilly to Miss M. Clark, 62 Stone Street, Newcastle on Tyne, on 19 July 1905: **'Sorry to hear that your mother is not well. Write and let me know if Bill's gear is done yet. Hope you are all well.'**

Gertie to Miss M. Neighbour, 11 The Parade, Old Road, Clacton-on-Sea, on 28 March 1906: **'Dear Missy, Thank you for P.C. Hope to see you soon. You are still in the same class at S.S. Weare. Having very cold weather now.'**

removed for scrap in the dark days of 1940. A wonderful domed sarcophagus with the marble urn, just inside the main entrance, is worthy of Highgate Cemetery. It is to H. T. Baker. My family's contribution, at the other end of the social scale, are the graves of my Winton grandfather, Robert George Legg (1873-1915) and grandmother, the former Miss Alice Jane Kearley (1872-1930) from Ridge in the Isle of Purbeck.